THE OFFICIAL TRUCK HANDBOOK

This handbook is only a guide. For official purposes, please refer to the Ontario Highway Traffic Act and regulations, the Dangerous Goods Act and Federal Motor Vehicle Transport Act.

For more information about driver licensing, visit www.mto.gov.on.ca.

To request a copy of this book in an alternate format, contact Publications Ontario at 1-800-668-9938 or (416) 326-5300 or on the Internet at www.publications.serviceontario.ca

Disponible en français
Demandez le « Guide official des Camions »

Driving is a privilege — not a right

Introduction

The Ministry of Transportation (MTO) is committed to making Ontario's roads safer for everyone. Ontario is a leader in truck safety standards and enforcement with some of the toughest safety laws in North America. The province has almost 75,000 commercial carriers actively operating on Ontario's roadways. Even though truck traffic has increased with Ontario's growing economy, there has been a long-term decline in fatal collisions involving large trucks, thanks to the collective efforts of government, police, industry, safety-minded organizations and conscientious drivers.

It takes skill to operate a commercial vehicle. A driver must have knowledge of vehicle maintenance, as well as a thorough understanding of the mechanical components of the vehicle — such as the brakes and the wheels. Drivers also need to know the law governing trucks, and they are expected to demonstrate safe driving practices.

This handbook is designed to help people applying for a class A or D driver's licence. It contains the information you need to meet the standards for those licences, and sets out the skills you will be expected to perform during a driving test. It also outlines the many safety initiatives the ministry has introduced and details the best practices for safe and responsible operation of a commercial vehicle.

CONTENTS

GETTING YOUR
LICENCE

I. Legislation

These Acts and regulations govern truck driving in Ontario.

1. The Highway Traffic Act (HTA) and regulations govern the driver, the vehicle and equipment, weight and size of loads, and the hours of service that a truck driver can operate.

2. The Dangerous Goods Act regulates the transportation of dangerous goods, including required documentation, handling, safety markings (labels and placards) and the certification of drivers.

3. The Motor Vehicle Transport Act (Federal) regulates the for hire transportation of goods and people.

Transporting Dangerous Goods

There are nine classes of dangerous goods ranging from corrosives and flammable liquids to environmentally hazardous materials. Drivers transporting dangerous goods must receive training from their current employer. The employer determines the level of training required. Once training is successfully completed, the employer issues the driver a certificate that they must carry when transporting dangerous goods.

For further information on dangerous goods training, visit the Transport Canada website: www.tc.gc.ca.

Driver's Licence Classification Chart

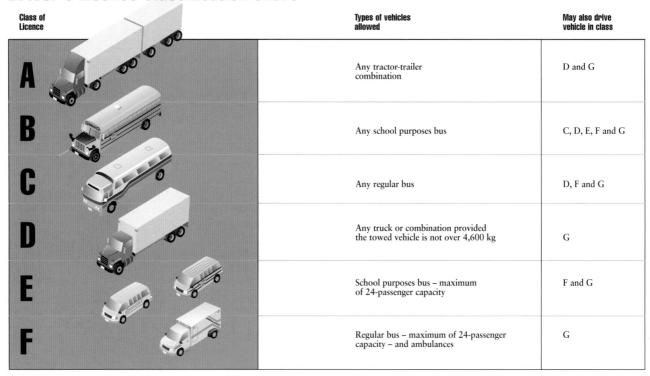

Class of Licence	Types of vehicles allowed	May also drive vehicle in class
A	Any tractor-trailer combination	D and G
B	Any school purposes bus	C, D, E, F and G
C	Any regular bus	D, F and G
D	Any truck or combination provided the towed vehicle is not over 4,600 kg	G
E	School purposes bus – maximum of 24-passenger capacity	F and G
F	Regular bus – maximum of 24-passenger capacity – and ambulances	G

Diagram 1-1a

Driver's Licence Classification Chart

Class of Licence	Types of vehicles allowed	May also drive vehicle in class
G	Any car, van or small truck or combination of vehicle and towed vehicle up to 11,000 kg provided the towed vehicle is not over 4,600 kg	
G1	Level One of graduated licensing. Holders may drive Class G vehicles with an accompanying fully licensed driver with at least four years' driving experience. Subject to certain conditions.	
G2	Level Two of graduated licensing. Holders may drive Class G vehicles without accompanying driver but are subject to certain conditions.	
M	Motorcycles, including limited-speed motorcycles (motor scooters) and motor-assisted bicycles (mopeds). Holders may also drive a Class G vehicle under the conditions that apply to a Class G1 licence holder.	
M1	Level One of graduated licensing for motorcycles, including limited-speed motorcycles (motor scooters) and motor-assisted bicycles (mopeds). Holders may drive a motorcycle under certain conditions.	
M2	Level Two of graduated licensing for motorcycles, including limited-speed motorcycles (motor scooters) and motor-assisted bicycles (mopeds). Holders may drive a motorcycle but only with a zero blood alcohol level. Holders may also drive a Class G vehicle under the conditions that apply to a Class G1 licence holder.	
M with L condition	Holders may operate a limited-speed motorcycle or moped only	May operate a limited speed motorcycle or moped only
M2 with L condition	Holders may operate a limited-speed motorcycle or moped only	May operate a limited speed motorcycle or moped only

Diagram 1-1b

A "Z" air brake endorsement is required on a driver's licence to operate any air brake equipped motor vehicle.

II. Definitions

Commercial motor vehicle: any motor vehicle with a permanently attached truck or delivery body, including ambulances, hearses, casket wagons, fire apparatus, buses and tractors used for hauling loads.

Gross weight: the combined weight of vehicle and load.

Registered gross weight: the weight for which a permit has been issued under the HTA; the fee for the permit is based upon the weight of the vehicle or combination of vehicles and load.

Manufacturers' gross vehicle weight rating (MGVWR): the gross weight as specified by the manufacturer; often attached as a decal or plate on the cab of a vehicle.

Motor vehicle: an automobile, motorcycle, motor assisted bicycle and any other vehicle propelled or driven other than by muscular power. Not included are the cars of electric or steam railways or other motor vehicles running only upon rails; motorized snow vehicles; traction engines; farm tractors; or road-building machines.

Semi-trailer: a trailer designed to be operated with the forward part of its body or chassis resting upon the body or chassis of a towing vehicle.

Trailer: a vehicle drawn, propelled or moved by a motor vehicle. The definition does not include farm implements, mobile homes, motor vehicles, side cars attached to motorcycles, or any device not designed to transport persons or property. A trailer is considered a separate vehicle and not part of the motor vehicle by which it is drawn.

Vehicle: a motor vehicle, trailer, traction engine, farm tractor, road-building machine or any vehicle drawn, propelled or driven by any kind of power, including muscular power. The definition does not include motorized snow vehicles or the cars of electric or steam railways running only upon rails.

Self-propelled implement of husbandry: a self-propelled vehicle used specifically in farming, such as a farm tractor.

III. A and D licence classes and requirements

The Driver's Licence Classification Chart on pages 8 to 9 shows you what class of licence you need to drive different types of vehicles. A licensed driver wishing to learn to operate a truck or tractor-trailer must hold a class G or higher driver's licence and be accompanied by a driver who holds a valid class D or class A licence respectively. Your driving competence will be assessed in a road test held at a DriveTest Centre; or an employer or community college authorized by the Ministry of Transportation (known as a Recognized Authority) may assess you on the road test and issue a certificate of driving competence for classes A, B, C, D, E, F and M. You may then obtain the appropriate driver's licence from the ministry.

The class A driver's licence allows you to drive a motor vehicle and towed vehicles where the towed vehicles exceed a total gross weight of 4600 kg (10,000 lb); and vehicles included in classes D and G. A class A licence does not permit you to drive a bus carrying passengers, a motorcycle or a moped.

The class D driver's licence allows you to drive a motor vehicle exceeding 11,000 kg (24,000 lb) gross weight or registered gross weight, or any combination of motor vehicle exceeding a total gross weight or registered gross weight of 11,000 kg (24,000 lb) and towed vehicle not exceeding a total gross weight of 4600 kg (10,000 lb). It also allows you to operate vehicles in class G. A class D licence does not permit you to drive a bus carrying passengers, a motorcycle or a moped.

Minimum requirements for Class A or D driver's licence application:

An applicant for a class A or D driver's licence must:
• Be at least 18 years of age

• Hold a valid Ontario class G or higher licence or equivalent
• Pass a test of operating knowledge of large trucks and tractor trailers
• Meet vision standards
• Provide a satisfactory medical certificate on application and periodically thereafter
• Demonstrate driving competence during a road test while driving the following types of vehicles:
  - For class D – a motor vehicle exceeding 11,000 kg (24,000 lb) gross weight or registered gross weight
  - For class A – a motor vehicle and towed vehicle where the towed vehicle exceeds a total gross weight of 4600 kg (10,000 lb)

Medical certificate

When applying for a class A or D licence, you must provide a completed satisfactory ministry medical certificate. Blank medical forms can be obtained from any DriveTest Centre in Ontario.

Your medical practitioner or optometrist is required by law to report to the licensing authorities any physical, neurological, cardio-vascular or other medical condition that might affect your safe operation of a motor vehicle.

Your application will be refused if your physical or medical condition does not meet the standards outlined in the regulations of the Highway Traffic Act.

Knowledge test checklist

Before taking the class A or D knowledge test, make sure you have studied the Official Truck Handbook.

Bring the following items to the test:

- 2 pieces of identification or Ontario Driver's Licence
- Complete medical report form
- Money for test fees – cash, debit or credit card

- Glasses or contact lenses (if you need to wear them to read or write)

Class A or D road test

All road tests have a set time frame. Before you begin your test, the examiner will inform you of the amount of time you have to complete each part of the test. The examiner will explain the test and you are to follow her or his instructions. The examiner is not allowed to coach you during the test, so if you have any questions, ask them before you begin.

On the road test:

- You will be required to demonstrate a daily trip inspection commonly known as a circle check. (See pages 19 to 20). You will be required to name the item of equipment checked, and briefly describe its condition.
- Class A applicants may be required to uncouple and couple the units of

the combination vehicle, or explain the procedures to the examiner.
- You will be required to drive in traffic and handle the vehicle safely.
- You may be required to reverse the vehicle into a parking bay or marked area.

Class A or D road test checklist

- Study the Official Truck Handbook before the test.
- Study the operating manual for the vehicle to be used for the road test.
- Bring the appropriate type of vehicle, in good working order, to the test.
- Bring glasses or contact lenses if you need to wear them to drive. (If your current licence is conditional on wearing corrective lenses, you cannot drive without wearing them.)

Commercial Vehicle Operator Registration (CVOR)

The Commercial Vehicle Operator Registration (CVOR) system is one method of monitoring the performance of commercial vehicle operators. An operator is the person responsible for the operation of a commercial motor vehicle including the conduct of the driver and the carriage of goods or passengers.

Under CVOR, operators of buses with a seating capacity of 10 or more and commercial motor vehicles with a registered or actual gross weight of over 4500 kg must obtain a CVOR certificate. Operators may obtain a CVOR certificate by submitting a CVOR application to the Ministry of Transportation. There is no charge for the initial registration.

Operators of ambulances, fire trucks or other emergency vehicles; hearses; motor homes; buses used for personal transporta-tion; vehicles leased for less than 30 days for personal use; and empty vehicles while using dealer plates or in-transit permits are not required to obtain a CVOR certificate.

Each CVOR certificate has a unique nine-digit CVOR number. In addition to proof of insurance and vehicle registration, a legible copy of the certificate must be carried in the applicable vehicles at all times and be presented to police and MTO enforcement personnel on request. The original should be kept in a safe place since there is a replacement fee if it is lost, stolen or destroyed.

The CVOR record contains information that includes all convictions (such as for speeding, load being overweight, having safety defects, failing to produce a valid CVOR certificate), reportable collisions, detentions and defaulted fines associated with the operator/carrier (regardless of the person charged). All items remain on the operator's CVOR record for five years from the date of the conviction.

If an operator's record becomes unacceptable, the ministry sends a warning letter to the operator or requests that the operator attend a meeting to discuss the record. If the operator's record does not improve, the ministry may impose sanctions including the cancellation or suspension of the CVOR certificate; or the limitation of fleet size through the use of fleet limitation certificates.

Size and weight limits for commercial motor vehicles

Commercial motor vehicles are restricted in width to a limit of 2.6 m (8.53 ft). Exceptions are made for specialized equipment such as traction engines, threshing machines and snow removal equipment. Mirrors are not included when determining the width of a commercial vehicle.

Semi-trailers are limited to a length of 14.65 m (48 ft) or 16.15 m (53 ft) if the trailer and tractor meets special requirements.

No combination of vehicles is permitted to exceed a length of 23 m (74.75 ft) except double trailer combinations which meet special requirements for both trailers and the tractor.

All vehicles, including loads, are limited to a height of 4.15 m (13.6 ft).

You cannot operate a vehicle or combination of vehicles on a highway when its gross weight exceeds the maximum weight permitted under Part VII of the Highway Traffic Act and its regulations. To determine the gross allowable weight of a commercial vehicle several factors must be considered, including the number of axles, the size of the tires, the type of suspension, the distance between the axles, the type of load carried (aggregate or non-aggregate load) and the weight allowed on the steering axle.

Several formulas are used to determine the maximum allowable gross weight. These include calculating the sum of the weights allowed on each axle, the registered gross vehicle weight (RGW), or the weight prescribed in regulations under the Highway Traffic Act. Once these weights have been determined, the lower figure of these is the maximum gross allowable weight.

Drivers, operators and shippers are all responsible for the weight of the commercial vehicle and any may be charged with an offence.

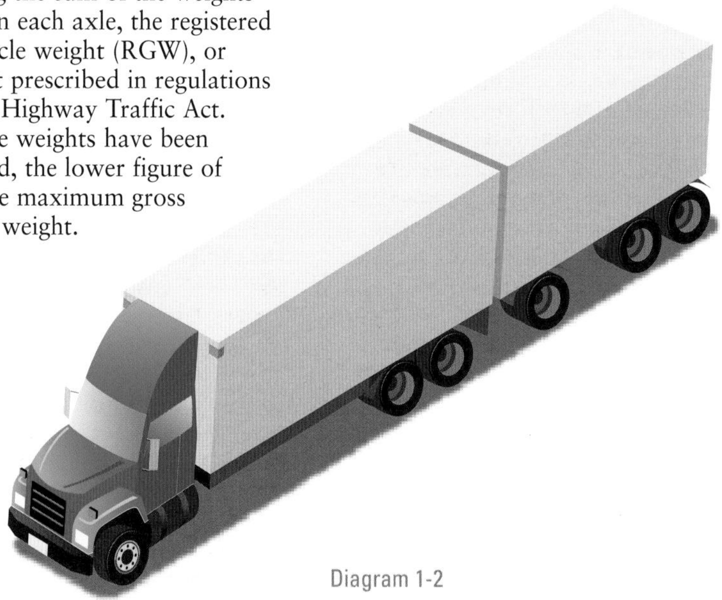

Diagram 1-2

IV. Vehicle safety, maintenance and inspections

Ministry of Transportation inspection stations

The Ministry of Transportation monitors the condition of commercial motor vehicles operating in Ontario and, when necessary, takes corrective action. One method of accomplishing this task is through vehicle inspections, which can be performed by ministry enforcement staff or police officers. Ministry enforcement staff perform inspections at truck inspection stations.

Truck inspection stations are found at various highway locations in Ontario. Signs indicate whether or not a station is open. If a station is open, trucks must enter and stop for inspection.

Vehicles and loads are checked for weight, height, length, width and axle spacing. Registration permits and licences are checked to ensure that a "for hire" carrier has the authority to transport the goods carried.

Driver licences are also checked for validity and proper class of licence for the vehicle.

Drivers are required to produce documents to show that they meet regulatory and legislative requirements such as daily trip inspections, log books indicating hours worked, and proof of commercial vehicle operator registration.

Vehicles are subject to safety checks (of brakes, lights, couplings for example). In addition to permanent truck inspection stations, mobile inspection units may be set up for varying lengths of time at any location.

Any police officer or appointed ministry officer may require you to drive to the nearest inspection station. If requested, you must assist in the inspection of the vehicle. Inspections may be done on a highway at any time.

If you refuse or fail to proceed to a weigh scale when requested, you are guilty of an offence and liable to a fine of $200 to $1,000. You may also have your licence suspended for up to 30 days.

Also, drivers who refuse or fail to redistribute or remove part of a load, or make arrangements to do so; or obstruct a weighing, measuring or examination, are guilty of an offence and liable to a fine of $100 to $200.

Tires and wheels

Another important component of vehicle safety is tires and wheels. You must check the tires and wheels of your vehicle as part of the pre-trip inspection to ensure they meet safety standards. For example, you must check your tires to ensure they have appropriate tread depth; and check your wheels to ensure they are securely attached. The rear tire of a motor vehicle must have more than 1.5 mm (0.05 in) of tread measured in two adjacent tread grooves. The front tires of a motor vehicle with a gross vehicle rating of more than 4500 kg must have at least 3 mm (0.12 in) of tread measured in two adjacent tread grooves.

It is also a good safety practice to inspect the wheels, wheel fasteners and tires after having new tires or wheels installed. Wheel manufacturers recommend having wheel fasteners rechecked between 80 km and 160 km after installation.

Wheels and tires must be installed by a qualified installer.

Cargo securement

As the driver, you are responsible for making sure the load is evenly balanced and properly secured against shifting. Any cargo that breaks loose or shifts during a sudden stop or sharp turn could cause a collision. All loads carried on a motor vehicle or trailer must be bound, covered or otherwise securely fastened or loaded such that no portion of the load can fall off the vehicle or trailer.

The Highway Traffic Act states that any load overhanging the rear of a vehicle by 1.5 m (5 ft) or more should be marked by a red light when lights are required (one-half hour before sunset to one-half hour after sunrise) and, at all other times, by a red flag or red marker.

Before moving a load, you should know the type of cargo you are carrying. Many commodities now being hauled require safety devices for the driver such as protective bulkheads or special lading. Before starting a trip or after unloading, check that van doors are latched or that racks, tarps and other equipment are properly secured.

Ontario has adopted National Safety Code (NSC) Standard 10 for Cargo Securement, developed and published by the Canadian Council for Motor Transport Administrators (CCMTA). Standard 10 provides detailed instructions for operators and drivers to follow when securing different types of loads to commercial vehicles. Every commercial vehicle carrying cargo on Ontario's roads must comply with the rules set out for cargo securement in this national standard. The standard was developed to increase both

Diagram 1-3

public safety and the safety of commercial vehicle drivers carrying loads. To read NSC Standard 10 for Cargo Securement visit CCMTA's website at www.ccmta.ca. See also Ontario Regulation 363/04 "Security of Loads" in the Highway Traffic Act at www.e-laws.gov.on.ca.

Annual inspection certificate

Operators are responsible for having each of their vehicles and trailers inspected each year by a licensed motor vehicle inspection mechanic. The mechanic checks to ensure that the vehicle or trailer is in compliance with all maintenance requirements and component performance standards detailed in the applicable regulations and schedules of the Highway Traffic Act.

If the vehicle/trailer is in compliance with all requirements, the mechanic, or another person authorized by the inspection station, completes an inspection certificate for it. The certificate comes with a corresponding decal, which indicates the vehicle type, as well as the month and year of the inspection. The mechanic, or other authorized person, places the decal on the outside lower left corner of the windshield or left side of the truck cab, or on the outside surface on the front left side of a trailer, semi-trailer or trailer converter dolly.

Drivers are also responsible for ensuring the vehicle they are driving is fit for highway use. As part of your daily trip inspection, check the date on the inspection certificate decal on the vehicle and/or trailer to ensure that the decal is still valid.

V. Daily trip inspection — classes A and D

Drivers play an important part in making sure that trucks and buses using Ontario highways are in good operating condition. The most effective method for drivers to determine that their vehicle is in safe operating condition is to do a daily vehicle inspection (also known as a circle check or a pre-trip inspection) before starting the day's trip.

Not only is it good safety practice, the daily trip inspection is a requirement of the Highway Traffic Act. Drivers must, by law, inspect their vehicles and be capable of determining if they are in a safe operating condition. A driver is required to complete a vehicle inspection every 24 hour period and monitor the vehicle's condition throughout the trip.

A driver is not permitted to drive a truck unless the driver or another person has, within the previous 24 hours, conducted a Schedule 1

inspection of the vehicle and completed an inspection report.

The inspection is conducted in accordance with an inspection schedule. The schedule provides a list of vehicle systems and components that a driver is required to inspect and provides a list of defects to guide and assist the driver.

The inspection schedule divides defects into two categories, major and minor. When a minor defect is identified, the driver must record the defect on the inspection report and report the defect to the operator. Drivers are not permitted to drive a vehicle with a major defect.

Drivers must carry both the current inspection report and the inspection schedule. Electronic reports and schedules are permitted.

The circle check or daily trip inspection in this book shows the absolute minimum inspection that must be performed as part of the driver testing procedure. For the full inspection schedules outlining all major and minor defects, which all commercial vehicle drivers are required to complete daily, refer to the Ontario Regulation 199/07 "Commercial Motor Vehicle Inspections" in the Highway Traffic Act at www.e-laws.gov.on.ca.

Upon identifying a safety defect, found either during the daily trip inspection, or during the trip itself, you must report the condition of the defect to the operator as soon as possible. Major defects must be repaired before you operate the vehicle again.

In cases where serious infractions are discovered, the vehicle is taken out of service. For less serious infractions, such as broken clearance lights, drivers should report the condition to the operator so that repairs can be made in a timely manner.

The most common reason for taking a commercial vehicle out of service is for out-of-adjustment air brakes. Other reasons include insecure loads, defective lights or tires, and broken springs. It is therefore very important that drivers also complete a proper air brake pre-trip inspection as described in The Official Air Brake Handbook before starting the day's trip. In addition to being unsafe, out of adjustment air brakes may result in a vehicle being detained and the operator's CVOR certificate may be cancelled or suspended.

Note: You cannot adjust your own air brakes unless you have either completed an approved air brake adjustment course or you are a certified mechanic.

The circle check

Diagram 1-4 shows a systematic circle check you should make. Details of the check can change according to the type of vehicle, but generally the principle of making a complete circle should be followed.

Some points to look out for are given in the sample.

As part of the road test, you will be expected to do the following:
- check fuel tank and fuel cap
- adjust seat and mirrors
- start engine
- check horn, wipers and all gauges and ensure that the low pressure warning device is operating
- while air pressure is building up, check emergency equipment
- when maximum pressure is gained, check for air leaks
- check all braking systems (refer to page 28)
- apply brakes, checking for pressure to drop (brake adjustment)

- turn on lights (lowbeam), put on left signal
- all lights
- wheel lugs, nuts and tires
- air hoses and electric lines to trailer (class A only)
- suspension and frame
- tailgate, trailer doors or tarp tie-downs
- trailer dolly wheels (class A only)
- fifth wheel (class A only)
- dimmer switch operation, put on right signal
- check signal lights and high-beam headlights
- clean glass and mirrors

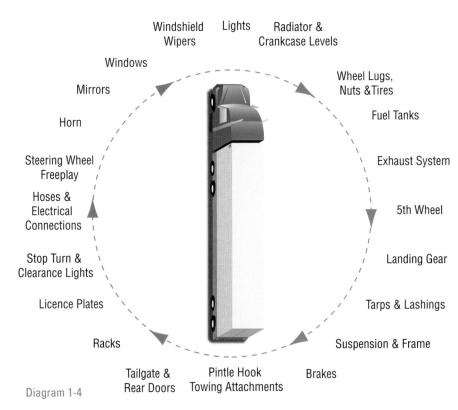

Windshield Wipers Lights Radiator & Crankcase Levels

Windows

Mirrors

Horn

Steering Wheel Freeplay

Hoses & Electrical Connections

Stop Turn & Clearance Lights

Licence Plates

Racks

Tailgate & Rear Doors

Pintle Hook Towing Attachments

Brakes

Wheel Lugs, Nuts & Tires

Fuel Tanks

Exhaust System

5th Wheel

Landing Gear

Tarps & Lashings

Suspension & Frame

Diagram 1-4

Uncoupling and coupling of combinations (class A only)

Uncoupling

1. Secure tractor and block trailer wheels if necessary; make certain trailer spring brakes are applied.
2. Check to see if the ground is firm enough to support landing gear. If necessary use planks or pads.
3. Lower trailer landing gear using low gear, if equipped, far enough to pick up the weight of trailer to the proper height for uncoupling, and secure the handle.
   Take care not to raise the trailer so high that no weight is on the fifth wheel, and avoid uncoupling with the trailer so low as to make re-coupling difficult or impossible. If the trailer has two-speed crank gear, place it in low range and stow the crank securely.
4. Release the secondary lock and pull the fifth wheel locking handle as far as it will go into the open position.

5. Start the tractor and pull ahead until the trailer upper plate slips to the lower part of the fifth wheel just above the chassis of the tractor. Stop and secure the tractor in this position.
6. Close the air lines either by cocks at the rear of the tractor cab, or the control valve on the dash.
7. Disconnect the supply or emergency air line from the trailer supply or emergency coupling; secure it to the dummy coupler on the rear of the cab.
8. Disconnect the light cord from the socket on the trailer; hang it on the rear of the cab.
9. Disconnect the service air line from the trailer service coupling; secure it to the dummy coupler on the rear of the cab.
10. Get back in the tractor and pull ahead slowly until the two units are separated.

Coupling

Be sure the fifth-wheel jaws are fully opened and the fifth wheel is tilted back so that hook-up can be made without damage. Make a visual inspection of the condition of the king pin and the fifth wheel. If the tractor is not equipped with a trailer hand valve or an emergency control valve, the trailer wheels must be blocked.

1. Back the tractor so the fifth-wheel slot is in line with the trailer kingpin.
2. Stop the tractor just as the fifth wheel makes contact with the trailer.
3. Secure the tractor and check to see the trailer is secured against movement before coupling.
4. Connect the brake lines and light cord to the trailer before coupling.
5. Open cocks or actuate the control valve on the dash in the cab to charge the trailer air system.
6. Release the trailer hand control valve and listen for exhausting air

to determine whether the trailer brakes are operating.

7. Be sure the trailer brake lines are properly connected. These are the standard colours usually used in the trucking industry.
   RED is supply or emergency
   BLUE is service

8. Before backing under the trailer, check the height of the trailer in relation to the fifth wheel. The trailer should be at a height where moderate resistance is met as the fifth-wheel contacts the trailer plate.

9. Back slowly under the trailer. See that firm contact is made between the fifth wheel and the upper plate on the trailer. Continue backing until you hear the jaws lock.

To test hook-up

Place the transmission in reverse and then partially release the clutch to move the power unit backward in a short, sharp motion. This is known as "hitting the pin."

Depress the clutch and place the transmission in the lowest forward gear. If the vehicle is equipped with a trailer hand control, pull it down to set trailer brakes to keep the unit from rolling. If there is no hand control, set the trailer parking brake.

Try to pull forward against the pin.

Check coupling (visual inspection)

- Leave the cab and look under the front of the trailer to be sure the upper plate of the trailer is resting firmly on the fifth wheel. If any space appears, the coupling is not secure.
- Be sure the fifth-wheel release lever is in locked position and the secondary lock, if there is one, is engaged.
- From behind the tractor, see that the jaws are completely closed.

Raise the landing gear after checking the hook-up and before moving the unit. Be sure the gear is fully raised. If you use a two-speed crank gear, place it in low range, and stow the crank securely.

VI. Hours of service

As of January 1, 2007, new hours of service came into effect for all drivers of commercial motor vehicles. This section provides an overview of the basic rules. All the details of the hours of service requirements are contained in the Highway Traffic Act in Ontario Regulation 555/06.

Drivers required to comply with hours of service regulations

The Hours of Service regulations apply to drivers of the following types of vehicles:

- Commercial motor vehicles having gross weight or registered gross weight over 4500 kilograms
- Buses, School Buses and School-purposes buses

Exemptions to hours of service regulations

Drivers of the following types of vehicles are not required to comply with the Hours of Service regulations:

- Commercial motor vehicles, other than buses, having gross weight or registered gross weight of not more than 4,500 kilograms;
- Commercial motor vehicles leased for no longer than thirty days by an individual;
- Commercial motor vehicles, operated under dealer or service permits, that are not transporting passengers or goods;
- Commercial motor vehicles operated under the authority of In-transit permits;
- Two or three axle commercial motor vehicles transporting primary farm, forest, sea or lake products;
- Mobile cranes;
- Pick-up trucks, being used for personal purposes, which have a manufacturer's gross vehicle weight rating of 6,000 kilograms or less;
- Tow trucks;
- Motor homes;

- Municipal buses operated as part of a public transit service;
- Buses used for personal purposes without compensation;
- Vehicles being used by a police officers;
- Cardiac arrest vehicles;
- Vehicles engaged in providing relief in emergencies; and
- Ambulances, fire apparatus, hearses or casket wagons.

Duty Status

The new rules define four categories of duty time for commercial vehicle drivers:

1. Off-duty time, other than time spent in a sleeper berth;
2. Off-duty time spent in a sleeper berth;
3. On-duty time spent driving; and
4. On-duty time, other than time spent driving.

On duty activities include driving, as well as performing any other activities for the operator, such as inspecting, cleaning or repairing your vehicle; travelling as a co-driver (not including when in sleeper berth); loading and unloading the vehicle; waiting at inspections, for unloading or loading to be completed, or because of an unforeseen occurrence such as an accident.

These four categories are used to determine the minimum off-duty required and the maximum on-duty times allowed for commercial vehicle drivers.

Hours of service requirements

1. Daily requirement*

- A driver must have 10 hours off-duty in a day;
- A driver cannot drive more than 13 hours in a day; and
- A driver cannot drive after 14 hours on-duty in a day.

* Some exceptions apply, refer to Ontario Regulation 555/06

2. Mandatory off-duty time

- After a period of at least 8 hours off-duty, a driver cannot drive more than 13 hours;
- After a period of at least 8 hours off-duty, a driver cannot drive after having been on-duty for 14 hours; and
- After a period of at least 8 hours off-duty, a driver cannot drive after 16 hours has elapsed.

3. Cycle requirement

- An operator shall designate a cycle for the driver to follow;
- There are two cycles available, a 7-day cycle or a 14-day cycle.
- In a period of 7 consecutive days, a driver cannot drive after having been on-duty for 70 hours;
- In a period of 14 consecutive days, a driver cannot drive after having been on-duty for 120 hours. Drivers following this cycle shall not drive after accumulating 70 hours on-duty without having

taken 24 consecutive hours of off-duty time.
- On any day, all drivers must have a period of at least 24 consecutive hours off-duty in the preceding 14 days.

4. Cycle reset/switching

- A driver may only switch the cycle they are on if they start a new cycle.
- To start a new cycle, a driver on the 7-day cycle must take 36 consecutive hours off-duty.
- To start a new cycle, a driver on the 14-day cycle must take 72 consecutive hours off-duty.

5. Daily log requirement

A daily log may be handwritten, computer generated or made by means of a recording device. The daily log must contain the following information:
- Driver's name
- Date

- Name of the driver's co-drivers, if any
- Start time of the day being recorded, if the day does not start at midnight
- Cycle that the driver is following
- Odometer reading, at the start of the day
- Number plate of each commercial motor vehicle to be driven and each trailer
- Name of the operator
- Address of the driver's home terminal and of the principal place of business of the operator
- Graph grid as illustrated in Form 1 of the regulation (not required for Recording Device).
- Start and end times for each duty status during the day
- Location where the driver's duty status changes
- Total time spent in each duty status during the day
- Odometer reading at the end of the day

- Total distance driven by the driver
- Driver's signature

6. Daily log exemption

A driver is not required to keep a daily log if the driver:

- Drives the commercial motor vehicle solely within a radius of 160 kilometres of the location at which the driver starts the day;
- Returns at the end of the day to the same location from which he or she started; and
- Only works for one operator that day.

If a driver is not required to keep a daily log the operator shall keep a record for the day showing:

- Date, driver's name and the location where the driver starts and ends the day
- Cycle that the driver is following

- Hour at which each duty status starts and ends
- Total number of hours spent in each duty status

These rules will help keep Ontario's roads safe by allowing commercial drivers to get the rest they need in order to safely operate their vehicles. For more details about the hours of service requirements, visit the MTO website at www.mto.gov.on.ca, or refer to the Highway Traffic Act at www.e-laws.gov.on.ca.

Chapter 1 — Summary

By the end of this chapter you should know:

- The different licence classifications and what types of vehicles they permit you to drive
- The requirements you must meet to obtain a truck driver's licence
- The requirements for Commercial Vehicle Operator Registration (CVOR) and vehicle documentation
- The size and weight limits for commercial motor vehicles
- The requirements for truck inspections, vehicle maintenance and inspection stations
- The requirements for vehicle loads and load security
- The requirements for daily trip inspection or circle checks
- The hours of service requirements for all commercial vehicle drivers

DRIVING—CLASSES A AND D

Starting the engine

1. Engage the parking brake, adjust the choke, depress the clutch pedal, and place the transmission in neutral.
2. Turn on the ignition; operate the starter.
3. Control the engine with the foot throttle until it is running smoothly.
4. Check the gauge for the proper oil pressure.
5. On vehicles with air brakes, the air pressure gauge should register sufficient pressure before moving. The audible air warning buzzer must have stopped sounding and/or the warning light must be off.

Note: For more information on air brakes, see The Official Air Brake Handbook.

Putting vehicle into motion

When starting to move, gradually release the clutch and at the same time release the hand control valve or parking brake. At the same time, the engine must be speeded up gradually on some vehicles to prevent stalling. Check the brakes immediately after you have the vehicle underway, within at least 15 m (50 ft).

Transmissions

- It is your responsibility to be thoroughly familiar with transmission shift patterns and shifting procedures. We recommend that you study the truck manufacturer's operating manual.
- When you start to move, put the vehicle in the lowest gear ratio available.

- Do not shock-load the drive-line through rapid operation of the clutch. Take care when applying power to move heavy loads uphill.
- Do not allow the clutch to slip: it will, generate excessive heat, cause the clutch to drag and bring on premature clutch failure.

Remember: co-ordinated clutch operation and smooth transmission shifting will prolong the life of any vehicle.

Some vehicles are equipped with a clutch brake. When driving them, the clutch pedal should not be depressed all the way to the floor when shifting, except at a stop. To re-enter low gear, depress the pedal to the floor to produce an easy, quiet engagement into low gear, with the vehicle at rest.

Inter-axle differential lock
The inter-axle differential lock is used on vehicles with tandem rear axles. Differential lock is controlled by a lever or push-pull control valve on the instrument panel.

This feature can be in only two positions—lock or unlock— as indicated.

Periodically, the valve should be operated to make sure it moves freely; normally the valve should be kept in the unlock position.

Use the lock position only when you approach conditions where one or both wheels of an axle may slip. The valve locks the differential and causes it to act as a "through drive," transmitting power equally to both axles. Avoid unnecessary use of differential lock since it will result in tire wear and axle strain.

Caution: You should not activate the differential lock when the wheels are actually spinning.

Note: Proper operating instructions vary from manufacturer to manufacturer.

Refer to your owner's manual for further instructions.

Brake inspection
While drivers are not expected to be able to service a disabled braking system, you should be knowledge-able enough to pinpoint the trouble. You should always carry out the following inspection routines as part of your daily trip inspection.
1. **Hydraulic brakes**
   (without power assist):
   - Apply brakes moderately and hold.
   - If the pedal shows a steady drop, the vehicle should be taken out of service and the system inspected professionally.
2. **Hydraulic brakes**
   (with power assist):
   - With the engine stopped, pump the brake pedal several times to eliminate power assist.
   - Apply brakes moderately.

- Start the engine (the pedal should drop slightly and stop).
- If the pedal continues to drop or does not drop (no power assist) stop the engine. The vehicle should be taken out of service and the system inspected professionally.

Use of brakes

Apply steady pressure at the beginning of a stop, then ease off as the vehicle slows. Just before the vehicle comes to a complete stop, release the brakes enough to avoid a jerk and rebound, then apply the brakes again to hold the vehicle while stopped.

You should not fan your brakes (alternately apply and release them) except on slippery pavement where this type of braking (also called threshold braking) gives better control, reduces danger of skidding and gives a shorter stop. Fanning reduces air pressure and serves no

useful purpose on dry pavement and fanning on a long downhill grade may reduce air pressure below the minimum pressure needed for proper brake operation.

Take great care to avoid excessive use of brakes on long downgrades, as overheated brakes are dangerously inefficient. Use engine compression as the principal means of controlling speed on long grades. If possible, you should use the same gear in descending a long grade as you would climbing it. Make your gear selection before descending a grade to minimize the chance of missing a shift.

If the low air pressure warning device operates at anytime, stop immediately in the safest available place and correct the loss of air pressure before proceeding.

If brakes should fail on a level road, you should downshift and use engine compression to slow the vehicle. If a shorter stopping

distance is necessary, use the tractor and trailer emergency brakes, if fitted, to stop. You should not drive the vehicle again until repairs have been made.

In a combination of vehicles such as a truck-tractor and semi-trailer, trailer brakes are applied with the truck brakes using the foot control valve. This is known as balanced braking. The pressure applied on both the trailer and the truck-tractor brakes is the same. Trailer brakes may be applied independently by using the trailer hand valve. Pulling harder on the hand valve may increase the amount of pressure on the trailer brakes during a foot valve application.

Exercise care in braking a combination of vehicles on wet or slippery surfaces, or on a curve. Over-braking in these circumstances can result in skidding or jack-knifing. If the tractor is jack-knifing, i.e. if the tractor rear wheels slide sideways, apply the trailer brakes only. If the trailer rear wheels slide sideways, release all brakes and gradually apply the accelerator.

Emergency brakes (spring brakes) are installed on newer equipment. They apply automatically when the air pressure in the system drops below a predetermined level, usually at 138-311 kPa (25-45 psi).

Note: If you plan to operate a vehicle equipped with air brakes, refer to The **OFFICIAL AIR BRAKE HANDBOOK** for further information.

Parking

To ensure that a unit will stay in position when parked, take the following precautions:

1. Set parking brakes.

2. Block the unit by placing chocks or blocks on the rear wheel (front and back of wheel) on one or both sides of the unit or trailer.

3. Under no circumstances should a driver use the trailer hand valve, or the tractor protection valve to hold a parked unit.

Stopping

Knowing how to stop safely and properly is an important driving skill. Safe and responsible drivers see stops ahead, check their mirrors, begin braking early and stop smoothly. Braking is easier when you sit properly. Use your right foot for both brake and gas pedals so you won't step on both pedals at the same time or activate your brake lights unnecessarily. Press the brake pedal firmly and evenly.

Shift into a lower gear when going down long, steep hills. This will help control your speed and you won't have to brake as sharply. Downshift before starting downhill since it may not be possible once you are going downhill. As a guide,

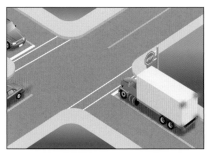

Diagram 2-1

Diagram 2-2

you should be in the same gear going downhill as uphill.

You must come to a complete stop for all stop signs and red traffic lights. Stop at the stop line if it is marked on the pavement. If there is no stop line, stop at the crosswalk, marked or not. If there is no crosswalk, stop at the edge of the sidewalk. If there is no sidewalk, stop at the edge of the intersection (See page 30). Wait until the way is clear before entering the intersection.

Stopping at railway crossings

All railway crossings on public roads in Ontario are marked with large red and white 'X' signs. Watch for these signs and be prepared to stop. You may also see yellow advance warning signs and large 'X' pavement markings ahead of railway crossings. Some railway crossings have flashing signal lights and some use gates or barriers to keep drivers from crossing the tracks when a train is coming. Some less travelled crossings have stop signs posted. Remember it can take up to two kilometres for a train to stop under full emergency braking. On private roads, railway crossings may not be marked, so watch carefully.

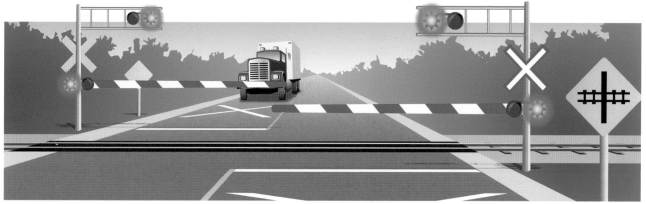

Diagram 2-3

When you come to a railway crossing, remember:

- Slow down, listen and look both ways to make sure the way is clear before crossing the tracks.
- If a train is coming, stop at least five metres from the nearest rail or gate. Do not cross the track until you are sure the train or trains have passed.
- Never race a train to a crossing.
- If there are signal lights, wait until they stop flashing and, if the crossing has a gate or barrier, wait until it rises, before you cross the tracks.
- Never drive around, under or through a railway gate or barrier while it is down, being lowered or being raised. It is illegal and dangerous.
- Avoid stopping in the middle of railway tracks; for example, in heavy traffic, make sure you have enough room to cross the tracks completely before you begin to cross.

- Avoid shifting gears while crossing tracks.
- If you get trapped on a crossing, immediately get everyone out and away from the vehicle. Move to a safe place and then contact authorities.
- Buses and other public vehicles are required to stop at railway crossings that are not protected by gates, signal lights, or a stop sign. School buses must stop at railway crossings whether or not they are protected by gates or signal lights. Watch for these buses and be prepared to stop behind them.

If you are approaching a railway crossing with a stop sign, you must stop unless otherwise directed by a flagman.

Stopping at school crossings

Where a school crossing guard displays a red and white stop sign

Diagram 2-4

you must stop before reaching the crossing and remain stopped until all persons, including the school crossing guard, have cleared your half of the roadway and it is safe to proceed. If you have any doubts on when it is safe to drive forward, wait until all the children and the guard have cleared the crossing. Drivers who don't follow the stopping requirements may be fined between $150 and $500 and get three demerit points.

Diagram 2-5

Stopping for school buses

School buses in Ontario come in a range of sizes. All are chrome yellow and display the words "School Bus."

You must stop whenever you approach a stopped school bus with its upper alternating red lights flashing, regardless of whether you are behind the bus or approaching it from the front. When approaching the bus from the front, stop at a safe distance for children to get off the bus and cross the road in front of you. If you are coming from behind the bus, stop at least 20 metres away. Do not go until the bus moves or the lights have stopped flashing.

If you are on a road with a median strip, only vehicles coming from behind the bus must stop. (A median is a physical barrier such as a raised, lowered, earth or paved strip constructed to separate traffic travelling in different directions. Vehicles cannot cross over a median strip.)

You must obey the school bus law on any road, no matter how many lanes or what the speed limit. Be prepared to stop for a school bus at any time, not just within school hours.

As well as the upper alternating red flashing lights, school buses use a stop sign arm on the driver's side of the bus. This arm, a standard stop sign with alternating flashing red lights at top and bottom, swings out after the upper alternating red lights begin to flash. Remain stopped until the arm folds away and all lights stop flashing.

It is illegal to fail to stop for a stopped school bus that has its red lights flashing. If you don't stop, you can be fined $400 to $2,000 and get six demerit points for a first offence. If you are convicted a second time within five years, the penalty is a fine of $1,000 to $4,000 and six demerit points. You could also go to jail for up to six months. In Ontario, school bus drivers and other witnesses can report vehicles that have illegally passed a school bus.

As the vehicle's registered owner, if the driver is not charged, the same fines may be applied to you. If you do not pay the fine, you will not be able to renew your vehicle permit.

Note: Watch for school buses near railway crossings. All school buses must stop at all railway crossings; however, the upper alternating red lights are not used for these stops.

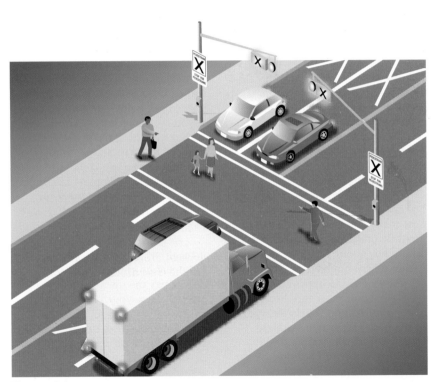

Diagram 2-6

Stopping for pedestrian crossovers

Pedestrian crossovers (commonly called crosswalks) are designated areas that allow pedestrians to safely cross roads where there are no traffic lights. Always watch for pedestrians and people using wheelchairs at these crossings. Pedestrians may push a button to make overhead yellow lights flash to warn drivers. Pedestrians should point across the road to show they want to cross before entering the roadway. Drivers, including cyclists, must stop and allow pedestrians to cross. Once people have cleared your side of the road, you can proceed with caution. Do not pass any vehicle within 30 metres of a pedestrian crossover. Never pass a vehicle that has stopped to allow pedestrians to cross the road.

Clearances

When you drive a larger vehicle, you must know the vehicle's height and width and watch for and obey clearance signs on bridges and underpasses. You must also remember that road repairs, rough roads, ice and floods may cause difficulty where clearance is otherwise normally adequate.

You must follow instructions on signs posted where dangerous conditions exist and obey regulations that ban trucks on certain highways, at certain times or on certain days.

Turns and steering

Turning a large vehicle requires more care and knowledge than turning a passenger car. Besides observing the general turn rules outlined in The Official Driver's Handbook, you must keep other factors in mind. For example, during a given turn of the steering wheel, the rear wheels follow a shorter path than those up front. Allow this on all turns so that your vehicle doesn't strike another vehicle or stationary object.

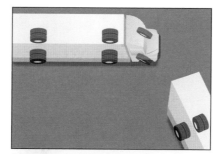

Diagram 2-7

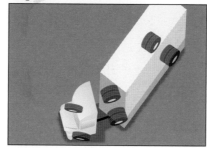

Diagram 2-8

Steering (forward) and off-track

The rear wheels of the vehicle do not pivot and therefore will not follow the same path as the front wheels. The greater the distance (wheel base) between the front wheels and the rear wheels of the vehicle, the greater the amount of "off-track." The off-track path has a shorter radius than the path of the front wheels.

On the open highway, you must lead your turning arc of the front wheels according to the sharpness of the curve and the amount of off-track of your vehicle (See Diagrams) A curve to the right requires keeping the front wheels close to the centre line to prevent dropping the rear wheels off the pavement. A curve to the left requires keeping the front wheels close to the right edge of the pavement to prevent the rear wheels from crossing into the other traffic lane.

A combination vehicle such as a semi-trailer unit has an off-track of the rear wheels of the tractor unit, and a greater off-track again of the rear wheels of a semi.

The combination unit of a truck-tractor and semi-trailer has different turning characteristics. These units have a turning radius and off-track pattern within each unit, but the amount of off-track depends upon the length of the combination and the wheel base of the units (See diagram).

Whenever possible, turns must be made from the proper lanes. When it becomes necessary for you to direct your vehicle over lane lines or centre lines to negotiate sharp turns, it is your responsibility to be sure that the movement can be made safely, without interfering with other traffic.

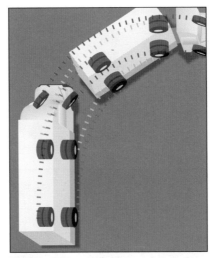

Diagram 2-9

Right turns

Right turns at intersections with vehicles that have a lot of off-track require you to lead the turning arc according to the amount of off-track, otherwise you run the risk of running the the rear

wheels of the unit over curbs and sidewalks.

Remember that you may need to proceed well into the intersection before beginning the turn. Generally, it is better to use more space from the road you are leaving than from the road you are entering. Move as close to the left side of the your lane as possible and then make the turn, using the space you need to complete the turn from the road you are entering. However, depending on the type of vehicle you are driving and the width of the road's lanes, you may have to cross the centre line or travel into the second traffic lane of the street entered.

If you are driving a tractor-trailer on a narrow street, for example, you will have to use some, or all, of the left lane in order to get your vehicle around the corner without the rear wheels of your unit going up on the curb. Use extreme caution and ensure the movement can be made safely.

When it is necessary to "block" off another traffic lane, make sure that smaller vehicles, motorcycles or cyclists are not attempting to move up along the right side of your vehicle. The critical point is reached when the tractor is at the sharpest point of the turn in relation to the trailer, because vision through your right rear view mirror is limited.

Left turns

You must be aware of and allow for any off-track when making a left turn. Unless you use your left outside mirror to monitor the trailer's path, the trailer might hit either a vehicle or a sign post on an island. You must turn the vehicle in a wide arc before bringing it back to its proper position after a left turn, just right of the centre line; then, as you increase speed, you can move, when it is safe, to the right lane.

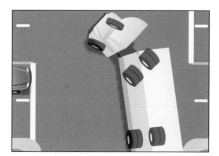

Diagram 2-10

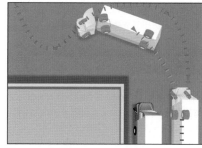

Diagram 2-11

Backing

Because of the hazards of backing, avoid it when possible. Planning your route in advance may eliminate the need for backing. If necessary, drive around the block if it will help you to avoid backing around a corner. Drive out into traffic rather than backing into traffic. Avoid entering the path of a reversing vehicle and do not stop or park behind a vehicle that may soon be reversed.

Backing a single unit vehicle is similar to backing a passenger vehicle; however, backing a tractor with a semi-trailer requires practice.

- Get out and walk around the vehicle to examine the area into which you must back. Look for overhead obstacles or wires, side clearances, pedestrians or objects in your path of travel.
- Whenever possible, back from the driver's side and start backing from as close to the dock as reasonably

possible. Although you may start with the vehicle in a straight line, it may be less difficult if you position your vehicle so that the trailer is angled in the direction you want it to take.

- Use both rear view mirrors. Even with two mirrors, vision is limited. There is always a blind spot to the rear that a mirror cannot reflect.
- Back **slowly**, in an S shaped curve, by first turning the tractor wheels in the opposite direction to that in which you want to move the rear of the trailer. Before you reach a jack-knife position, the tractor must follow in a track related to the track of the trailer (forming the bottom portion of the "S").
- Moving slowly, the tractor should follow the trailer until both tractor and trailer are straight. Once both are straight, you can continue to slowly ease up to the dock.

A responsible guide or flag person can help you by watching the area into which you are backing and by keeping an eye on your blind zone. This person should stand in a position to see both you and the area to the rear of your vehicle clearly, and warn you if pedestrians or vehicles move into your path as you back. This can help you make an easy approach to the dock.

Remember that back-up alarm devices do not relieve the driver of responsibility when reversing.

Backing from a Roadway into a Driveway

The hazards of backing are increased when backing into a hidden laneway or driveway from a road, especially at night. Avoid it when possible. As the driver, you are responsible for ensuring all precautions are taken when attempting to back into a driveway from the road. Most importantly, you must

be able to make this move safely for your own sake and for the safety of other drivers.

Use your judgement to determine if a guide or flag person, flares, markers or a blocker vehicle are required. Make yourself visible to other motorists.

Their safety and their lives depend on your judgement.

Chapter 2 — Summary

By the end of this chapter you should know:

- Where to position your vehicle when stopping at stop lights and stop signs
- The importance of stopping at railway crossings and how to position your vehicle to stop for them
- How and when to stop for school crossings and school buses
- How and when to stop for pedestrian crossovers
- The use of the transmission, differential lock and the braking system
- The importance of knowing your vehicle's height and width
- How to steer in forward, reverse and while turning
- The meaning of "off track" and where to position your vehicle on the road

Chapter 3

SAFE AND RESPONSIBLE DRIVING

I. Precautions

Observe the laws governing the operation of a motor vehicle scrupulously and make every effort to follow good driving practice and safety rules.

- Back a truck with the utmost care and caution. Use all rear view mirrors, turn and look back and, if possible, have someone give you directions. Back slowly and cautiously and watch traffic conditions around the vehicle at all times.
- Bad weather requires changing your driving procedures. Exercise exceptional care in such conditions.
- Adjust your speed to meet road, weather and traffic conditions.
- Never load a truck beyond its licensed capacity.
- Avoid situations that call for quick stops.
- Never allow an unauthorized person to occupy the driver's seat, operate the truck or any of its controls.

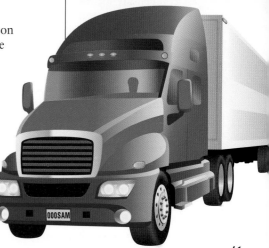

II. Driver conduct

Today's truck drivers are among the most visible citizens on the highways, and the motoring public tends to criticize some of their driving practices. So it's up to responsible truck drivers to influence the public's opinion. Be a defensive driver — anticipate what other drivers might do and compensate for them.

1. **Obstructing traffic:** Slowing down on hills is often unavoidable, but good drivers can reduce the delay to faster vehicles by being aware of the following traffic and pulling off the roadway when it is safe to do so, allowing faster traffic to pass. Never use your left-turn signals to tell following motorists it is safe to pass. It is against the law and tends to confuse other drivers, who may think you are signaling a left turn or lane change.

2. **Improper passing:** Some truck drivers switch on their turn signals and immediately pull out into traffic when the traffic stream is too close and dense. Another complaint is the practice of pulling out to pass another large vehicle on a multiple lane highway when the difference in speed is so small that the manoeuvre obstructs following traffic for an unreasonable period of time. Avoid these errors.

3. **Bluffing:** Drivers who use the large size of their vehicles to intimidate others and force their way through traffic may create serious hazards.

4. **Following:** When a number of trucks pull onto a highway after a stop, drivers should do so at intervals that will allow them to leave sufficient space. Commercial motor vehicles must maintain a minimum distance of at least 60 m (200 ft) between themselves and other vehicles when on a highway at a speed exceeding 60 km/h (40 mph) except when overtaking and passing another motor vehicle.

III. Sharing the Road

Sharing the road with smaller vehicles

Be aware that most drivers of smaller vehicles do not understand what it is like to drive a large vehicle such as a tractor-trailer. Many do not realize that a tractor-trailer needs twice as much stopping distance as the average car, and takes much longer to get up to normal driving speed. Many drivers also feel nervous when a large vehicle comes up behind or beside them, and this may cause them to make sudden or unexpected moves.

Here are some tips for sharing the road with smaller vehicles:

1. **Following:** It is very dangerous to follow too closely behind another vehicle. If something unexpected occurs, you will not have enough room to stop safely. Also, be aware that a large vehicle looming up closely behind may intimidate drivers of small vehicles.

2. Being passed: Be courteous when smaller, faster vehicles are trying to pass you. Slow down enough to allow the vehicle to fit in quickly and safely in front of you.

3. Signalling: Signal your intentions clearly before turning, slowing or stopping so that other drivers will have adequate time to react appropriately.

4. Turning: Many drivers of smaller vehicles do not understand how much room large vehicles need in order to make a turn. Drivers of smaller vehicles will often drive up into the large vehicle's turning space, not realizing until too late that the large vehicle needs that space to complete the turn. Always check to make sure a vehicle has not moved up into your turning space before completing your turn.

Sharing the road with motorcycles, limited-speed motorcycles or mopeds

Motorcycles, limited-speed motorcycles and mopeds are harder to see because of their size. Drivers of these vehicles may make sudden moves because of uneven road surfaces or poor weather conditions. Because they are less protected, they are more likely to be injured in a collision.

Motorcycles and mopeds that cannot keep up with traffic should drive as close as possible to the right edge of the road; however, remember that these vehicles have the right to use the whole lane.

Since many motorcycle turn signals do not automatically shut off, be careful when turning left in front of an oncoming motorcycle with its turn signal on. Make sure the motorcyclist is actually turning; he or she may have just forgotten to switch off the turn signal.

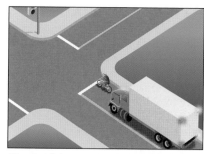

Diagram 3-1

Diagram 3-2

Sharing the road with cyclists

Bicycles and mopeds that cannot keep up with traffic are expected to keep to the right of the lane; however, they can use any part of the lane if necessary for safety, such as to avoid potholes and sewer grates. Cyclists need a metre on either side of themselves as a safety zone. When passing a cyclist, allow at least one metre between your truck and the cyclist. If the lane is too narrow to share, change lanes to pass the cyclist. When turning right, signal and check your mirrors and the blind spot to your right to make sure you do not cut off a cyclist. When parked on the side of the street, look behind you and check your mirrors and blinds spots for a passing cyclist before opening a door.

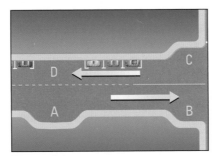

Diagram 3-3

A Mid-block indented bays
B An indentation before an intersection
C An indentation after an intersection
D Bus stops between legally parked cars

Sharing the road with municipal buses

Many municipal roadways have special indented stopping areas for municipal buses, called bus bays, where passengers can get on and off. There are three types of bus bays:
- Mid-block indented bays
- Indentations immediately before and after intersections

- Bus stop areas between two designated parking areas

When a bus in a bus bay begins flashing its left turn signals, indicating that it is ready to leave the bus bay, and you are approaching in the lane adjacent to the bus bay, you must allow the bus to re-enter traffic.

Sharing the road with farm machinery

Farm machinery moves quite slowly compared to other road users. Most tractors and combines have a maximum speed of 40 km/h, but travel at less than 40 km/h when towing implements or wagons. Farm machinery is often oversized, wide or long or both, making it difficult for the driver to see vehicles coming up from behind. Farmers often turn directly into fields rather than roads or lanes, or move from lane to lane. Remember that it is common for farmers to be on the roads after dark during peak planting and harvesting seasons.

Farm machinery on the road must display an orange and red slow-moving vehicle sign on the rear of the vehicle. The sign warns other drivers that the vehicle is travelling at 40 km/h or less. If you see one of these signs, slow down and be cautious. Stay well back and do not pass until it is safe to do so. (See the slow-moving vehicle sign on page 81.)

Sharing the road with pedestrians

Pay special attention to pedestrians, whether they are crossing roads in traffic, walking or jogging alongside roads, or using crosswalks or cross-overs (generally known as crossings). Watch for children. Drive slowly and cautiously through school zones, residential areas and any other area where children may be walking or playing. You never know when a child might dart out from between parked cars or try to cross a street without checking for oncoming traf-

fic. Be very cautious at twilight when children may still be playing outside, but are very difficult to see. Watch out for Community Safety Zone signs as they indicate areas where the community has identified that there is a special risk to pedestrians.

Elderly pedestrians, or those with disabilities, need extra caution and courtesy from drivers, as they may be slow in crossing the road. Be alert for pedestrians who are blind, visually impaired, hearing impaired, people in wheelchairs or people walking slowly due to some other physical impairment and give them appropriate consideration. Pedestrians who are blind or visually impaired may use a white cane or guide dog to help them travel safely along sidewalks and across intersections. Caution signs are posted in some areas where there is a special need for drivers to be alert.

Diagram 3-4

Persons operating mobility devices (motorized wheelchair and medical scooters) are treated the same way as pedestrians. Usually these operators will travel along a sidewalk but if there is no sidewalk available, persons using a mobility device should travel, like pedestrians, along the left shoulder of the road-way facing oncoming traffic.

Some streetcar stops have a special safety island or zone for passengers getting on and off. Pass these safety islands and zones at a reasonable speed. Always be ready

Diagram 3-5
in case pedestrians make sudden or unexpected moves.

Yielding the right-of-way

There are times when you must yield the right-of-way. This means you must let another person go first. Here are some rules about when you must yield the right-of-way:

At an intersection without signs or lights, you must yield the right-of-way to any vehicle approaching from the right (Diagram 3-4).

At an intersection with stop signs at all corners, you must yield

Diagram 3-6
the right-of-way to the first vehicle to come to a complete stop. If two vehicles stop at the same time, the vehicle on the left must yield to the vehicle on the right (Diagram 3-5).

At any intersection where you want to turn left or right, you must yield the right-of-way. If you are turning left, you must wait for approaching traffic to pass or turn and for pedestrians in your path to cross. If you are turning right, you must wait for pedestrians to cross (Diagram 3-6).

Diagram 3-7
A yield sign means you must slow down or stop if necessary and yield the right-of-way to traffic in the intersection or on the intersecting road.

When entering a road from a private road or driveway, you must yield to vehicles on the road and pedestrians on the sidewalk (Diagram 3-7).

You must yield the right-of-way to pedestrians crossing at specially marked pedestrian crossings or crossovers (Diagram 3-8).

Diagram 3-8

Remember, signalling does not give you the right-of-way. You must make sure the way is clear.

10 ways you can help make Ontario's roads the safest in North America

1. Don't drink and drive. Don't drive when you're taking medication that will affect your driving

2. Always wear your seat belt

3. Obey the speed limits. Slow down when road and weather conditions are poor

4. Don't take risks: don't cut people off in traffic, make sudden lane changes or run yellow lights

5. Don't drive when you're tired, upset or sick

6. If you're in doubt, let the other driver go first — yield the right-of-way

7. Keep a safe distance between your vehicle and the one ahead

8. Avoid distractions such as loud music and cell phones

9. Check your mirrors frequently; always check your blind spot before you change lanes

10. Check traffic in all directions before going into an intersection

IV. Driving at night and in bad weather

At night and in weather conditions such as rain, snow or fog, you cannot see as far ahead, even with headlights. Slow down when driving at night, especially on unlit roads, and whenever weather conditions reduce your visibility.

Overdriving your headlights

You are overdriving your headlights when your stopping distance is farther than you can see with your headlights. This is a dangerous thing to do because you may not give yourself enough room to make a safe stop. Reflective road signs can mislead you as well, making you believe you can see farther than you really can. This may cause you to overdrive your headlights if you are not careful.

Glare

Glare is dazzling light that makes it hard for you to see and be aware of what others around you are doing.

It can be a problem on both sunny and overcast days, depending on the angle of the sun's rays and your surroundings. Glare can also be a problem at night when you face bright headlights or see them reflected in your mirrors.

When meeting oncoming vehicles with bright headlights at night, look up and beyond and slightly to the right of the oncoming lights. In daytime glare, use your sun visor or use a pair of good quality sunglasses. When you enter a tunnel on a bright day, slow down to let your eyes adjust to the reduced light. Remove your sunglasses and turn on your headlights.

Cut down glare at night by following the rules of the road for vehicle lights. Use your lowbeam headlights within 150 m (500 ft) of an oncoming vehicle or when following a vehicle within 60 m (200 ft). On country roads, switch to lowbeams when you come to a

curve or hilltop so you can see oncoming headlights and won't blind oncoming drivers. If you can't see any headlights, switch back to highbeams.

Fog

Fog is a thin layer of cloud resting on the ground. Fog can reduce visibility for drivers, resulting in difficult driving conditions.

The best thing to do is to avoid driving in fog. Check weather forecasts and if there is a fog warning, delay your trip until it clears. If that is not possible or you get caught driving in fog, there are a number of safe driving tips you should follow. If visibility is decreasing rapidly, move off the road and into a safe parking area to wait for the fog to lift.

Tips for driving safely in fog

Before you drive — and during your trip — check weather forecasts. If there is a fog warning, delay your trip until it clears, if possible. If you are caught driving in fog, follow these safe driving tips:

DO:

- Slow down gradually and drive at a speed that suits the conditions.
- Make sure the full lighting system of your vehicle is turned on.
- Use your lowbeam headlights Highbeams reflect off the moisture droplets in the fog, making it harder to see.
- If you have fog lights on your vehicle, use them, in addition to your lowbeams. They could save your life.
- Be patient. Avoid passing, changing lanes and crossing traffic.
- Use pavement markings to help guide you. Use the right edge of the road as a guide, rather than the centre line.

- Increase your following distance. You will need extra distance to brake safely.
- Look and listen for any hazards that may be ahead.
- Reduce the distractions in your vehicle. For example, turn off the cell phone. Your full attention is required.
- Watch for any electronically-operated warning signs.
- Keep looking as far ahead as possible.
- Keep your windows and mirrors clean. Use your defroster and wipers to maximize your vision.
- If the fog is too dense to continue, pull completely off the road and try to position your vehicle in a safe parking area. Turn on your emergency flashers.

DON'T:

- Don't stop on the travelled portion of the road. You could become

the first link in a chain-reaction collision.
- Don't speed up suddenly, even if the fog seems to be clearing. You could find yourself suddenly back in fog.
- Don't speed up to pass a vehicle moving slowly or to get away from a vehicle that is following too closely.

REMEMBER:

- Watch your speed. You may be going faster than you think. If so, reduce speed gradually.
- Leave a safe braking distance between you and the vehicle ahead.
- Remain calm and patient. Don't pass other vehicles or speed up suddenly.
- Don't stop on the road. If visibility is decreasing rapidly, pull off the road into a safe parking area and wait for the fog to lift.
- When visibility is reduced, use your lowbeam lights.

Rain

Rain makes road surfaces slippery, especially as the first drops fall. With more rain, tires make less contact with the road. If there is too much water or if you are going too fast, your tires may ride on top of the water, like water skis. This is called hydroplaning. When this happens, control becomes very difficult. Make sure you have good tires with deep tread, and slow down when the road is wet.

Rain also reduces visibility. Drive slowly enough to be able to stop within the distance you can see. Make sure your windshield wipers are in good condition. If your wiper blades do not clean the windshield without streaking, replace them.

In rain, try to drive on clear sections of road. Look ahead and plan your movements. Smooth steering, braking and accelerating will reduce the chance of skids. Leave more space between you

and the vehicle ahead in case you have to stop. This will also help you to avoid spray from the vehicle ahead that can make it even harder to see.

Avoid driving in puddles. A puddle can hide a large pothole that could damage your vehicle or its suspension, or flatten a tire. The spray of water could splash nearby pedestrians or drown your engine, causing it to stall. Water can also make your brakes less effective.

Flooded roads

Avoid driving on flooded roads — water may prevent your brakes from working. If you must drive through a flooded stretch of road, test your brakes afterwards to dry them out.

Test your brakes when it is safe to do so by stopping quickly and firmly. Make sure the vehicle stops in a straight line, without pulling to one side. The brake pedal should

feel firm and secure, not spongy — that's a sign of trouble.

If you still feel a pulling to one side or a spongy brake pedal even after the brakes are dry, you should take the vehicle in for repair immediately.

Skids

A skid happens when your wheels slide out of control on a slippery surface. Skids can involve the front, rear or all wheels and can cause your vehicle to jack-knife. Most skids result from driving too fast for road or traffic conditions. Sudden, hard braking, going too fast around a corner or accelerating too quickly can cause your vehicle to skid or roll over.

If you do find yourself in a skid, look where you want the vehicle to go and steer in that direction. Be careful not to oversteer. If you are on ice, skidding in a straight line, step on the clutch or shift to neutral.

Threshold Braking — Threshold braking should bring you to a reasonably quick controlled stop in your own lane, even in slippery conditions. Brake as hard as you can without locking up or skidding the wheels. Press down on the brake pedal, trying to get as much braking power as possible. Then, if you feel any of the wheels locking up, release the brake pressure slightly and re-apply. Don't pump the brakes. Continue braking this way until you have brought the vehicle to a complete stop. Some vehicles have anti-lock brake systems that give you a maximum threshold stop automatically.

Anti-lock Brakes — If your vehicle has an anti-lock braking system, practice emergency braking to understand how your vehicle will react. It is a good idea to practice doing this under controlled conditions with a qualified driving instructor.

Anti-lock braking systems, which are also called ABS, are designed to sense the speed of the wheels on a vehicle. An abnormal drop in wheel speed, which indicates potential wheel lock, causes the brake force to be reduced to that wheel. This is how the anti-lock braking system prevents tire skid and the accompanying loss of steering control. This improves vehicle safety during heavy brake use or when braking with poor traction.

Although anti-lock braking systems help to prevent wheel lock, you should not expect the stopping distance for your vehicle to be shortened. Under normal driving conditions, on clean dry roads, you will notice no difference between vehicles with anti-lock braking and vehicles without anti-lock braking.

Drivers unfamiliar with anti-lock braking are usually surprised by the vibration that happens the first time they brake hard in an emergency.

Make sure you know what to expect so you can react quickly and effectively in an emergency.

Snow

Snow may be hard-packed, slippery as ice, rutted, full of hard tracks and gullies, or smooth and soft. Look ahead and anticipate what you must do based on the snow conditions. Slow down on rutted snowy roads. Avoid sudden steering, braking or accelerating that could cause a skid.

Whiteouts

Blowing snow may create whiteouts where snow completely blocks your view of the road. When blowing snow is forecast, drive only if necessary and with extreme caution.

Tips for driving in blowing snow and whiteout conditions

Before you drive — and during your trip — check weather forecasts and road reports. If there is a weather warning, or reports of poor visibility and driving conditions, delay your trip until conditions improve, if possible. If you get caught driving in blowing snow or a whiteout, follow these safe driving tips:

DO:
- Slow down gradually and drive at a speed that suits the conditions.
- Make sure the full lighting system of your vehicle is turned on.
- Be patient. Avoid passing, changing lanes and crossing traffic.
- Increase your following distance. You will need extra space to brake safely.
- Stay alert. Keep looking as far ahead as possible.
- Reduce the distractions in your vehicle. Your full attention is required.

- Keep your windows and mirrors clean. Use defroster and wipers to maximize your vision.
- Try to get off the road when visibility is near zero. Pull into a safe parking area if possible.

DON'T:
- Don't stop on the travelled portion of the road. You could become the first link in a chain-reaction collision.
- Don't attempt to pass a vehicle moving slowly or speed up to get away from a vehicle that is following too closely.

REMEMBER:
- Watch your speed. You may be going faster than you think. If so, reduce speed gradually.
- Leave a safe braking distance between you and the vehicle ahead.

- Stay alert, remain calm and be patient.
- If visibility is decreasing rapidly, do not stop on the road. Look for an opportunity to pull off the road into a safe parking area and wait for conditions to improve.
- If you become stuck or stranded in severe weather, stay with your vehicle for warmth and safety until help arrives. Open a window slightly for ventilation. Run your motor sparingly. Use your emergency flashers.
- Be prepared and carry a winter driving survival kit that includes items such as warm clothing, non-perishable energy foods, flashlight, shovel and blanket.
- It is important to look ahead and watch for clues that indicate you need to slow down and anticipate slippery road conditions.

Ice

As temperatures drop below freezing, wet roads become icy. Sections of road in shaded areas or on bridges and overpasses freeze first. It is important to look ahead, slow down and anticipate ice.

If the road ahead looks like black and shiny asphalt, be suspicious. It may be covered with a thin layer of ice known as black ice. Generally, asphalt in the winter should look gray-white in colour. If you think there may be black ice ahead, slow down and be careful.

Snow plows

Snow removal vehicles are equipped with flashing blue lights that can be seen from 150 m (500 ft).

Flashing blue lights warn you of wide and slow-moving vehicles. Some snow plows have a wing that extends as far as three metres to the right of the vehicle. On freeways, several snow plows may be staggered across the road, clearing all lanes at the same time by passing a ridge of snow from plow to plow. Do not try to pass between them. This is extremely dangerous because there is not enough room to pass safely, and the ridge of wet snow can throw your vehicle out of control.

V. Dealing with particular situations

Drowsy driving

Drowsiness has been identified as a causal factor in a growing number of collisions resulting in injury and fatality. Tired drivers can be as impaired as drunk drivers. They have a slower reaction time and are less alert.

Studies have shown that collisions involving drowsiness tend to occur during late night/early morning hours (between 2:00 a.m. and 6:00 a.m.) or late afternoon (between 2:00 p.m. and 4:00 p.m.) Studies also indicate that shift workers, people with undiagnosed or untreated sleep disorders, and commercial vehicle operators, are at greater risk for such collisions.

Always avoid driving when you are feeling drowsy. Scientific research confirms that you can fall asleep without actually being aware of it. Here are eight important warning signs that your drowsiness is serious enough to place you at risk:

- You have difficulty keeping your eyes open
- Your head keeps tilting forward despite your efforts to keep your eyes on the road
- Your mind keeps wandering and you can't seem to concentrate
- You yawn frequently
- You can't remember details about the last few kilometres you have travelled
- You are missing traffic lights and signals
- Your vehicle drifts into the next lane and you have to jerk it back into your lane
- You have drifted off the road and narrowly avoided a crash

If you have one of these symptoms, you may be in danger of falling asleep. Pull off the road and park your vehicle in a safe, secure place.

Use well-lit rest stops or truck stops on busy roads. Lock your doors, roll up your windows, and take a nap.

Stimulants are never a substitute for sleep. Drinks containing caffeine can help you feel more alert, but if you are sleep deprived, the effects wear off quickly. The same is true of turning up the volume of your radio or CD player and opening the window. You cannot trick your body into staying awake; you need to sleep. Remember, the only safe driver is a well-rested, alert driver.

Aggressive driving and road rage

Aggressive driving behaviours, such as tailgating, speeding, failing to yield the right of way and cutting in front of someone too closely, may cause other drivers to become frustrated and angry and lead to a road rage conflict between drivers. An angry driver may attempt dangerous retaliatory action. Avoid becoming angry on the road by following these tips:

- Know the warning signs of stress and combat them by getting fresh air, breathing deeply and slowly, and listening to relaxing music.
- Make a conscious decision not to take your problems with you when driving.
- If you are on a long trip, take a break from driving every few hours.
- Don't compete with another driver, or retaliate for what you believe to be inconsiderate behaviour.
- If someone else's driving annoys you, don't try to "educate" the person. Leave traffic enforcement to the police.
- Don't take other drivers' mistakes or behaviours personally.
- Avoid honking your horn at other drivers, unless absolutely necessary. A light tap on the horn is usually sufficient.

Remember that if you drive responsibly and courteously, you are less likely to spark a road rage situation.

- Plan your route in advance. Some of the most erratic and inconsiderate driving occurs when a driver is lost.
- Drive in a courteous and considerate manner.
- Yield the right-of-way when it is courteous to do so.
- Be polite and let other drivers in front of you when they are signalling that they would like to do so.
- If you make a mistake while driving, indicate that you are sorry. An apology can greatly reduce the risk of conflict.
- Don't return aggression. Avoid eye contact and do not gesture back. Keep away from erratic drivers.

If you are in a situation in which you feel threatened by another driver, do the following:

- Stay in your vehicle and lock the doors.
- If you have a cell phone, call police.
- Use your horn and signals to attract attention.
- If you believe you are being followed, do not drive home. Drive to a police station or a busy public place.

Workers on the road

Be extra careful when driving through construction zones and areas where people are working on or near the road.

When approaching a construction zone, slow down and obey all warning signs and people and/or devices that are directing traffic through the area. Municipalities can lower the speed limits in construction zones to increase safety for workers. Reduced speed limits come into effect once signs are posted in the area. In the construction zone, drive carefully and adjust your speed and driving to suit the conditions. Obey posted speed limits, do not change lanes, be ready for sudden stops and watch for workers and construction vehicles on the road and give them more room to ensure everyone's safety.

Traffic control workers control vehicle traffic in work zones and prevent conflicts between construction activity and traffic. Whether you are driving during the day or at night, watch for traffic control people and follow their instructions.

Treat people working on roads with respect and be patient if traffic is delayed. Sometimes traffic in one direction must wait while vehicles from the other direction pass through a detour. If your lane is blocked and no one is directing traffic, yield to the driver coming from the opposite direction. When the way is clear, move slowly and carefully around the obstacle.

Recent changes to the Highway Traffic Act have resulted in doubled fines for speeding in a construction zone when workers are present. It is also an offence to disobey **STOP** or **SLOW** signs displayed by a traffic control person or firefighter.

Animals on the road

Crashes involving animals (mainly moose and deer) are a growing problem. You may encounter domestic, farm or wild animals on the road anywhere in Ontario. The number of animals hit by vehicles increased from 7,388 in 1994 to 13,729 in 2003, an 86% increase over a 10-year period.

Many areas of the province have animal crossing signs that warn drivers of the danger of large animals (such as moose, deer or cattle) crossing the road.

Be cautious when you see these signs, especially during dusk to dawn hours when wild animals are most active.

To reduce your chances of hitting an animal:

- Reduce speed in darkness, rain and fog. These conditions can reduce your ability to see an animal on or near the road.
- Travel at a safe speed and stay alert. Driver inattention and speed are common factors in animal-vehicle crashes.
- Scan the road ahead from shoulder to shoulder. If you see an animal on or near the road, slow down and pass carefully, as they may suddenly bolt onto the road.
- Watch for shining eyes at the roadside. If you do see shining eyes, slow down and be ready to stop.
- Keep your windshield clean and headlights properly adjusted.

- Use high beams whenever possible and safe to do so and scan both sides of the road ahead.

If you see an animal:
- Slow down and sound your horn.
- Be alert for other animals which may be with the one you've seen.
- Don't try to drive around the animal. Animal movements are unpredictable.
- If you wish to watch an animal, find a safe place to pull completely off the road and park first. Do not park on the shoulder of the road, as other drivers may be distracted by the animal and hit your vehicle.
- Stay in your vehicle; getting out increases your chance of being hit by another vehicle.
- If you hit a deer or moose, report it to the local police service or the Ministry of Natural Resources. Do not try to move an injured animal.

Driver distractions

Driving is a job that requires your full attention every time you get behind the wheel. Any secondary activity will detract from your ability to drive properly and safely. You must reduce distractions and focus on your driving.

There are a number of possible driver distractions including:

- Using devices such as GPS systems, stereos, CD and DVD players, radios, cell phones, laptops, Personal Digital Assistants (PDAs) or MP3 players
- Reading maps, directions or other material
- Grooming (combing hair, putting on make-up or shaving)
- Eating or drinking
- Taking notes
- Talking with passengers
- Tending to children or pets
- Adjusting the controls in your vehicle (radio, CD player or climate control)
- Visual distractions outside your vehicle, such as collisions or police activity

Careless driving is a serious offence. Police can charge you with careless driving if you do not pay full attention to your driving. If you are convicted of careless driving, you will get six demerit points and can be fined up to $1,000 and sentenced to up to six months in jail. In some cases, your licence may be suspended for up to two years.

Tips to reduce driver distractions

- Attend to personal grooming and plan your route before you leave.
- Identify and preset your vehicle's climate control, radio and CD player.
- Make it a habit to pull over and park to use your cell phone or have a passenger take the call or let it go to voice mail.
- Put reading material away if you are tempted to read.
- Do not engage in emotional or complex conversations. Stress can affect your driving performance.
- When you are hungry or thirsty, take a break from driving.

Remember to focus on your driving at all times. A split-second distraction behind the wheel can result in injury or even death.

Emergency vehicles

Emergency vehicles include fire and police department vehicles, ambulances and public utility emergency vehicles.

Reacting to an Approaching Emergency Vehicle:

When you see red or red AND blue flashing lights or hear the bells or sirens of an emergency vehicle approaching from either direction, you must immediately slow down, move as far to the right side of the roadway as you can, and stop.

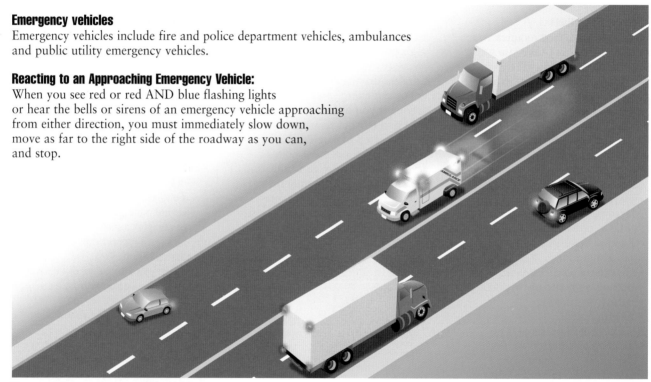

Diagram 3-9

Stay alert. When you see an approaching emergency vehicle with its lights or siren on, prepare to clear the way.

- React quickly but calmly. Don't slam on the brakes or pull over suddenly. Use your signals to alert other drivers you intend to pull over.
- Check your rear-view mirrors. Look in front and on both sides of your vehicle. Allow other vehicles to also pull over. Pull to the right and gradually come to a stop.
- Wait for the emergency vehicle to pass and watch for other emergency vehicles that may be responding to the same call. Check to make sure the way is clear and signal before merging back into traffic.
- Don't drive on or block the shoulder on freeways. Emergency vehicles will use the shoulder of the road if all lanes are blocked.

Never follow or try to outrun an emergency vehicle. It is illegal to follow within 150 metres of a fire vehicle or ambulance responding to a call in any lane going in the same direction.

Failing to pull over and stop for an approaching emergency vehicle can result in a conviction and a fine.

Note: Some fire fighters and volunteer medical responders may display a flashing green light when using their own vehicles to respond to a fire or medical emergency. Please yield the right-of-way to help them reach the emergency quickly and safely.

Take lights and sirens seriously. Clear the way! Pull to the right and stop. It's the law.

Approaching a stopped emergency vehicle with red or red AND blue flashing lights

When you see an emergency vehicle stopped with its red or red AND blue flashing lights in a lane or on the shoulder in your direction of travel, you must slow down and pass with caution. If the road has two or more lanes, you must move over into another lane to allow one lane clearance between your vehicle and the emergency vehicle, if it can be done safely. Failing to follow these rules can result in a conviction, demerit points on your driving record, a driver's licence suspension of up to two years and a fine of $400 to $2,000 for a first offence and $1,000 to $4,000 for a 'subsequent' offence. (a 'subsequent' offence is when you are convicted again within five years). The court can order you to spend up to six months in jail, or you may have to pay a fine or both.

VI. Dealing with emergencies

Emergency warning devices

Every commercial motor vehicle, on a provincial highway from one-half hour before sunset to one-half hour after sunrise, must have a sufficient number of:

- flares, lamps or lanterns capable of continuously producing two warning lights, each visible from a distance of at least 150 m (500 ft) for at least eight hours; or
- portable reflectors, during the time when lights are required.

Whenever any commercial motor vehicle or trailer is disabled during those hours and the vehicle cannot immediately be removed from the roadway, the driver is required to light flares, lamps or lanterns and place them or portable reflectors on the highway until they are no longer required. One of the devices must be approximately 30 m (100 ft) in front of the vehicle and one approximately 30 m (100 ft) to the rear and visible from at least 150 m (500 ft).

Even during daylight hours, if visibility is limited by fog, rain or snow, warning devices should be used.

Hills, curves, etc: You must not park or leave a vehicle on a roadway unless there is a clear view for at least 125 m (400 ft) in both directions. Whenever the view of a stopped vehicle is blocked by a hill, curve or other obstruction within 150 m (500 ft), an additional warning signal should be placed to give ample warning to other highway users.

Use caution in placing flares where fuel or flammable material has leaked.

Breakdown procedure

If a truck stalls or breaks down on the highway, the driver should quickly and calmly take the necessary actions to safeguard the vehicle and other motorists.

1. The truck should be brought to a stop as far off the roadway as safely possible.
2. Flares, lamps, lanterns or portable reflectors should be set out at a distance of approximately 30 m (100 ft) in advance of the vehicle and at a distance of approximately 30 m (100 ft) to the rear of the vehicle and visible for a distance of at least 150 m (500 ft).

Fire Precautions

Commercial vehicle drivers should know how to prevent fires and have a basic knowledge of fire fighting techniques. It's also essential to know what types of extinguisher or retardants to use on different types of fires.

Class A: fires include burning wood, paper, textiles, tires, etc.

Class B: fires include grease, oil, gasoline, solvents, paints, etc.

Class C: fires are those occurring in live electrical equipment

Class D: fires include burning metals such as magnesium, sodium, potassium etc. Only special compounds suitable to the combustible metal involved should be used to extinguish fires on these materials

Use all extinguishers according to the manufacturer's instructions. Some of the common causes for truck fires are:

- Running with a soft tire. Tire pressures should be checked at least every 160 km (100 mi);
- Overheated brakes, either from misuse or maladjustment. Check hub temperatures every time tires are checked;
- Leaking fuel system, carburetor, pump, filter, tanks or lines;

- Unequal distribution of load, causing trailer to lean and rub on tires;
- Careless smoking habits. Lighted cigarettes and cigars should always be butted in ashtrays, never thrown out windows. Never smoke while loading or unloading;
- Blocked air vents in a heated van can sometimes cause an explosion;
- Carelessly placed flares, lamps or fuses used in an emergency;
- Short circuits in the electrical system.

There are various other reasons for fires, such as leaking exhaust systems or those that have been installed too close to fuel lines or wooden body parts. Occasionally, spontaneous combustion may occur in a van or trailer. Drivers must always know the nature of their cargoes, so necessary fire control precautions can be taken.

When a fire occurs:

1. Stop the vehicle in a safe position away from buildings and other vehicles.
2. If it is a combination unit, uncouple the unit if possible.
3. If the fire occurs in or near a town, contact the fire department. Tell them what type of material is burning.
4. Based on the type of fire concerned, take all possible steps to extinguish it.
5. If the fire is thought to be due to a short-circuit, remove battery cables.
6. If the cargo is of an explosive nature, stop traffic and warn spectators to stay back.

In a collision where someone is injured

St. John Ambulance recommends that all drivers carry a well-stocked first aid kit and know how to use it. Consider reading a book about first aid or sign up for a first aid course. It could mean the difference between life and death in a collision.

Every driver involved in a collision must stay at the scene or return to it immediately and give all possible assistance. If you are not personally involved in a collision, you should stop to offer help if police or other help has not arrived.

In a collision with injuries, possible fuel leaks or serious vehicle damage, stay calm and follow these steps:

1. Call for help or have someone else call. By law, you must report any collision to the police when there are injuries or damage to vehicles or other property exceeding $1,000.

2. Turn off all engines and turn on emergency flashers. Set up warning signals or flares and have someone warn approaching drivers.

3. Do not let anyone smoke, light a match or put flares near any vehicle in case of a fuel leak. If a vehicle is on fire, get the people out and make sure everyone is well out of the way. If there is no danger of fire or explosion, leave injured people where they are until trained medical help arrives.

4. If you are trained in first aid, treat injuries in the order of urgency, within the level of your training. For example, clear the person's airway to restore breathing, give rescue breathing or stop bleeding by applying pressure with a clean cloth.

5. If you are not trained in first aid, use common sense. For example, people in collisions often go into shock. Cover the person with a jacket or blanket to reduce the effects of shock.

6. Stay with injured people until help arrives.

7. Disabled vehicles on the road may be a danger to you and other drivers. Do what you can to make sure everyone involved in a collision is kept safe.

In a collision where no one is injured

Follow these steps in a collision where there are no injuries:

1. If the vehicles can be moved, move them as far off the road as possible — this should not affect the police officer's investigation. This is especially important on busy or high speed roads where it may be dangerous to leave vehicles in the driving lanes. If you cannot move the vehicles off the road, set up warning signals or flares far enough away to give other traffic time to slow down or stop.

2. Call police (provincial or local, depending on where the collision takes place). By law, you must report any collision to the police-

where there are injuries or damage to vehicles or property exceeding $1,000.

3. Give all possible help to police or anyone whose vehicle has been damaged. This includes giving police your name and address, the name and address of the registered owner of the vehicle, the vehicle plate and permit number and the liability insurance card.

4. Get the names, addresses and phone numbers of all witnesses.

5. If damage is less than $1,000, you are still required by law to exchange information with anyone whose vehicle has been damaged. However, the collision does not have to be reported to the police.

6. Contact your insurance company as soon as possible if you intend to make a claim.

Chapter 3 — Summary

By the end of this chapter you should know:

- The rules of etiquette for driving a large vehicle
- The importance of sharing the road with other road users, especially small vehicles, cyclists and pedestrians
- The concept of right of way and common situations where you must yield to other road users
- How to identify and manage situations where your visibility may be reduced
- How weather conditions such as rain, flooded roads, snow and ice may affect your vehicle and your ability to control it
- What to do if your vehicle skids or if you encounter heavy snow, whiteouts or black ice
- Recognizing and sharing the road with snow removal vehicles
- Recognizing the signs of drowsiness and the importance of not driving when drowsy
- Recognizing the signs of aggressive driving both in yourself and other drivers; how to avoid road rage; and what to do if you find yourself in a situation involving aggressive driving or road rage
- How to manoeuvre your vehicle through construction zones
- What to do if you encounter animals on the road

- Things that may distract you when driving and how to minimize those distractions
- What to do when you encounter an emergency vehicle
- What to do in emergency situations when your vehicle stalls or breaks down
- How to prevent fires and basic fire fighting techniques
- The steps to take if you are involved in a collision with or without injuries

Traffic laws include the traffic signs and lights, pedestrian signals and pavement markings that tell drivers and other road users what they must do in certain situations. This chapter shows you what many of those signs, lights and markings look like and explains what they mean to drivers.

I. Signs

Traffic signs give you important information about the law, warn you about dangerous conditions and help you find your way. Signs use different symbols, colours and shapes for easy identification.

Here are some of the many signs you will see on Ontario roads:

 A stop sign is eight-sided and has a red background with white letters. It means you must come to a complete stop. Stop at the stop line if it is marked on the pavement. If there is no stop line, stop at the crosswalk. If there is no crosswalk, stop at the edge of the sidewalk. If there is no sidewalk, stop at the edge of the intersection. Wait until the way is clear before entering the intersection.

 A school zone sign is five-sided and has a blue background with white symbols. It warns that you are coming to a school zone. Slow down, drive with extra caution and watch for children.

A yield sign is a triangle with a white background and a red border. It means you must let traffic in the intersection or close to it go first. Stop if necessary and go only when the way is clear.

A railway crossing sign is X-shaped with a white background and red outline. It warns that railway tracks cross the road. Watch for this sign. Slow down and look both ways for trains. Be prepared to stop.

There are four other kinds of signs: regulatory, warning, temporary conditions and information and direction.

Regulatory signs

These signs give a direction that must be obeyed. They are usually rectangular or square with a white or black background and black, white or coloured letters.

A sign with a green circle means you may or must do the activity shown inside the ring.

A red circle with a line through it means the activity shown is not allowed.

Here are some common regulatory signs:

This road is an official bicycle route. Watch for cyclists and be prepared to share the road with them.

You may park in the area between the signs during the times posted. (Used in pairs or groups.)

Snowmobiles may use this road.

Do not enter this road.

 Do not stop in the area between the signs. This means you may not stop your vehicle in this area, even for a moment. (Used in pairs or groups.)

 Do not stand in the area between the signs. This means you may not stop your vehicle in this area except while loading or unloading passengers. (Used in pairs or groups.)

 Do not park in the area between the signs. This means you may not stop your vehicle except to load or unload passengers or merchandise. (Used in pairs or groups.)

 Do not turn left at the intersection.

 Do not drive through the intersection.

 Do not turn to go in the opposite direction. (U-turn)

 Do not turn right when facing a red light at the intersection.

 Do not turn left during the times shown.

 This parking space is only for vehicles displaying a valid Accessible Parking Permit.

 No bicycles allowed on this road.

67

No pedestrians allowed on this road.

 Do not pass on this road.

 These signs, above the road or on the pavement

1 **2** **3**

before an intersection, tell drivers the direction they must travel. For example: the driver in lane one must turn left; the driver in lane two must turn left or go straight ahead; and the driver in lane three must turn right.

 Keep to the right of the traffic island.

 Slow traffic on multi-lane roads must keep right.

SLOWER
TRAFFIC
KEEP
RIGHT

 Traffic may travel in one direction only.

 Speed limit changes ahead.

 The speed limit in this zone is lower during school hours. Observe the speed limit shown when the yellow lights are flashing.

MAXIMUM
40
km/h
WHEN
FLASHING

 This is a pedestrian crossover. Be prepared to stop and yield right-of-way to pedestrians.

PEDESTRIAN
X

NO
PASSING
HERE TO
CROSSING

This sign, above the road or on the ground, means the lane is only for two-way left turns.

This sign reserves curb area for vehicles displaying a valid Accessible Parking Permit picking up and dropping off passengers with disabilities.

These signs mean lanes are only for specific types of vehicles, either all the time or during certain hours. Different symbols are used for the different types of vehicles. They include: buses, taxis, vehicles with three or more people and bicycles.

Keep to the right lane except when passing on two-lane sections where climbing or passing lanes are provided.

STOP FOR SCHOOL BUS
WHEN SIGNALS FLASHING

Stop for school bus when signals are flashing.

STOP FOR SCHOOL BUS
WHEN SIGNALS FLASHING
BOTH DIRECTIONS

This sign is installed on multi-lane highways with no centre median divider. It informs drivers approaching from both directions that they must stop for a school bus when its signal lights are flashing.

No trucks in this lane.

No trucks over 6.5 metres in indicated lane.

No trucks over 6.5 metres in length in this lane.

Heavy trucks permitted on this roadway.

Road forks to the right.

No heavy trucks permitted on this roadway.

No heavy trucks permitted on this roadway between the hours of 7 p.m. – 7 a.m.

MAXIMUM WEIGHT 10 tonnes

No vehicles over 10 tonnes on this roadway.

LOAD RESTRICTION IN EFFECT 5 tonnes per axle

No vehicles that bear more than 5 tonnes per axle permitted on this roadway.

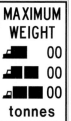

Indicates different weight restrictions for different types of heavy trucks for a bridge structure.

DANGEROUS GOODS ROUTE

Trucks carrying dangerous materials permitted on this roadway.

Trucks carrying dangerous materials permitted on this roadway.

Trucks carrying dangerous materials are not permitted on this roadway.

DANGEROUS GOODS CARRIERS PROHIBITED

No vehicles containing hazardous materials permitted on this roadway.

SCHOOL BUS LOADING ZONE →

School bus loading zone, proceed with caution.

TRUCKS ENTER INSPECTION STATION WHEN LIGHTS FLASHING

Trucks must enter inspection station when signals are flashing.

(407) ETR *Express Toll Route* Vehicles Over 5 Tonnes Must Have Valid Transponder

Any trucks over 5 tonnes must have a valid 407 transponder to use ETR.

Warning signs

These signs warn of dangerous or unusual conditions ahead such as a curve, turn, dip or sideroad. They are usually diamond-shaped and have a yellow background with black letters or symbols.

Here are some common warning signs:

USE LOWER GEAR

Trucks are advised to use a lower gear when travelling this portion of roadway.

ONE LANE ONLY WHEN USED BY TRUCKS

Indicates that horizontal clearance does not allow room for another vehicle when structure is being used by a truck.

 Maximum vertical clearance of 3.9 metres.

 Maximum vertical clearance of 3.9 metres under this obstruction.

 Indicates that an upcoming structure might not allow room for a tall vehicle; therefore, drivers of such vehicles should choose an alternate route.

 Tab indicates that sign has pertinence when lights are flashing.

 Trucks are advised to slow down around this curve due to its smaller radius.

 Trucks over 10 tonnes are advised not to use this roadway.

 Advises trucks to use caution if they are over indicated weight restrictions for their truck type.

 Indicates an upcoming truck-entrance and vehicles should be prepared to yield to trucks entering the roadway.

Indicates an upcoming bus entrance on the right and vehicles should be prepared to yield to buses entering the roadway.

 Indicates an upcoming fire truck entrance on the right and vehicles should be prepared to yield to trucks entering the roadway.

FIRE TRUCK ENTRANCE Indicates an upcoming fire truck entrance and vehicles should be prepared to yield to trucks entering the roadway.

SCHOOL BUS STOP AHEAD School bus stop ahead, proceed with caution.

 Narrow bridge ahead

 Road branching off ahead.

 Intersection ahead. The arrow shows which direction of traffic has the right-of-way.

 HIDDEN Drivers on the sideroad at the intersection ahead don't have a clear view of traffic.

 Pavement narrows ahead.

 Slight bend or curve in the road ahead.

73

Posted under a curve warning, this sign shows the maximum safe speed for the curve.

 The bridge ahead lifts or swings to let boats pass.

 Share the road with oncoming traffic.

 Sharp bend or turn in the road ahead.

 Paved surface ends ahead.

 Pavement is slippery when wet. Slow down and drive with caution.

 Chevron (arrowhead) signs are posted in groups to guide drivers around sharp curves in the road.

 Bicycle crossing ahead.

 Winding road ahead.

 Stop sign ahead. Slow down.

 Hazard close to the edge of the road. The downward lines show the side on which you may safely pass.

The road ahead is split into two separate roads by a median. Keep to the right-hand road. Each road carries one-way traffic.

 Right lane ends ahead. If you are in the right-hand lane you must merge safely with traffic in the lane to the left.

 Traffic lights ahead. Slow down.

 Steep hill ahead. You may need to use a lower gear.

 Two roads going in the same direction are about to join into one. Drivers on both roads are equally responsible for seeing that traffic merges smoothly and safely.

 Snowmobiles cross this road.

 Divided highway ends: traffic travels in both directions on the same road ahead. Keep to the right.

 Bump or uneven pavement on the road ahead. Slow down and keep control of your vehicle.

Railway crossing ahead. Be alert for trains. This sign also shows the angle at which the railway tracks cross the road.

Sharp turn or bend in the road in the direction of the arrow. The checkerboard border warns of danger. Slow down; be careful.

Deer regularly cross this road; be alert for animals.

Truck entrance on the right side of the road ahead. If the sign shows the truck on the left, the entrance is on the left side of the road.

Shows maximum safe speed on ramp.

Watch for pedestrians and be prepared to share the road with them.

Watch for fallen rock and be prepared to avoid a collision.

There may be water flowing over the road.

This sign warns you that you are coming to a hidden school bus stop. Slow down, drive with extra caution, watch for children and for a school bus with flashing red lights.

These signs warn of a school crossing. Watch for children and follow the directions of the crossing guard or school safety patroller.

High Occupancy Vehicle (HOV) signs

Only public vehicles such as buses, or passenger vehicles carrying a specified minimum number of passengers, may use this lane.

Vehicles cannot change lanes into or out of a high occupancy vehicle lane in this area.

Temporary condition signs

These signs warn of unusual temporary conditions such as road work zones, diversions, detours, lane closures or traffic control people on the road. They are usually diamond-shaped with an orange background and black letters or symbols.

Here are some common temporary condition signs:

Construction work one kilometre ahead.

Road work ahead.

Survey crew working on the road ahead.

Traffic control person ahead. Drive slowly and watch for instructions.

You are entering a construction zone. Drive with extra caution and be prepared for a lower speed limit.

Temporary detour from normal traffic route.

Flashing lights on the arrows show the direction to follow.

Pavement has been milled or grooved. Your vehicle's stopping ability may be affected so obey the speed limit and drive with extra caution. Motorcyclists may experience reduced traction on these surfaces.

Lane ahead is closed for roadwork. Obey the speed limit and merge with traffic in the open lane.

Closed lane. Adjust speed to merge with traffic in lane indicated by arrow.

Do not pass the pilot or pace vehicle bearing this sign.

Reduce speed and be prepared to stop.

Follow detour marker until you return to regular route.

Information and direction signs

These signs tell you about distances and destinations. They are usually rectangular with a green background and white letters. Other signs with different colours guide you to facilities, services and attractions.

Here are some common information and direction signs:

 Shows directions to nearby towns and cities.

 Shows the distances in kilometres to towns and cities on the road.

 Various exit signs are used on freeways. In urban areas, many exit ramps have more than one lane. Overhead and ground-mounted signs help drivers choose the correct lane to exit or stay on the freeway.

 Advance signs use arrows to show which lanes lead off the freeway. Signs are also posted at the exit.

 Sometimes one or more lanes may lead off the freeway. The arrows matching the exit lanes are shown on the advance sign in a yellow box with the word 'exit' under them.

 Freeway interchanges or exits have numbers that correspond to the distance from the beginning of the freeway. For example, interchange number 204 on Highway 401 is 204 kilometres from Windsor, where the freeway begins. Distances can be calculated by subtracting one interchange number from another.

The term 'VIA' is used to describe the roads that must be followed to reach a destination.

These signs change according to traffic conditions to give drivers current information on delays and lane closures ahead.

Shows off-road facilities such as hospitals, airports, universities or carpool lots.

Shows route to passenger railway station.

Shows route to airport.

Shows route to ferry service.

Shows facilities that are accessible by wheelchair.

Other signs

Here are some other common signs:

Oversize load sign

Vehicles and/or loads in excess of dimensions prescribed under Section 109 of the Highway Traffic Act must be marked with bright red or orange warning flags, which are at least 40 cm square, mounted to the extremities of the vehicle or load. The flag(s) must be kept in good and clean condition so as to not diminish their effectiveness.

In addition to flags, vehicles and/or loads must display on the front of the vehicle and the rear of the load, in a clearly visible position, either one of the two following signs: a sign visible for a distance of at least 150 metres bearing the words "OVERSIZE LOAD" in black letters at least 200 millimetres high on a yellow background; or, a "D" sign as illustrated below. When travelling at night, the sign must be made of high intensity retro-reflective material. The sign cannot obstruct lights or other safety devices on the vehicle or trailer; and it must be removed or covered when not in use.

The following is a diagram of a "D" sign.

Slow-moving vehicle sign

The slow-moving vehicle sign is orange with a red border. Motor vehicles moving slower than 40 km/h must have this sign on the rearmost part of the vehicle when it is being driven on a road, unless they are only crossing it.

Emergency response signs

Some information signs include a numbering system along the bottom of the sign to assist emergency vehicles in determining an appropriate route.

Bilingual signs

Watch for these signs when driving in designated bilingual areas. Read the messages in the language you understand best. Bilingual messages may be together on the same sign or separate, with an English sign immediately followed by a French sign.

II. Traffic lights

Traffic lights tell drivers and pedestrians what they must do at intersections and along roads. They tell road users when to stop and go, when and how to turn and when to drive with extra caution.

Green light

A green light means you may turn left, go straight or turn right after yielding to vehicles and pedestrians already in the intersection. When turning left or right you must yield the right-of-way to pedestrians crossing the intersection.

Yellow light

A yellow — or amber — light means the red light is about to appear. You must stop if you can do so safely; otherwise, go with caution.

Red light

A red light means you must stop. Bring your vehicle to a complete stop at the stop line if it is marked on the pavement. If there is no stop line, stop at the crosswalk, marked or not. If there is no crosswalk, stop at the edge of the sidewalk. If there is no sidewalk, stop at the edge of the intersection.

Wait until the light changes to green and the intersection is clear before moving through it.

Unless a sign tells you not to, you may turn right on a red light only after coming to a complete stop and waiting until the way is clear. You may also turn left on a red light if you are moving from a one-way road onto a one-way road, but you must come to a complete stop first and wait until the way is clear.

Lights and arrows to help turning vehicles

Flashing green lights and green arrows direct drivers who are turning.

Advance green light or arrow

When you face a flashing green light or a left-pointing green arrow and a green light, you may turn left, go straight ahead or turn right from the proper lane. This is called an advanced green light because oncoming traffic still faces a red light.

Pedestrians must not cross on a flashing green light unless a pedestrian signal tells them to.

Simultaneous left turn

When a left-turn green arrow is shown with a red light, you may turn left from the left-turn lane. Vehicles turning left from the opposite direction may also be making left turns because they too face a left-turn green arrow.

After the left-turn green arrow, a yellow arrow may appear. This means the green light is about to appear for traffic in one or both directions. Do not start your left turn. Stop if you can do so safely; otherwise, complete your turn with caution.

You can still turn left when the light is green, but only when the way is clear of traffic and pedestrians. If the light turns red when you are in the intersection, complete your turn when it is safe.

Pedestrians must not cross on a left-turn green arrow unless a pedestrian signal tells them to.

Transit priority signals

Traffic and pedestrians must yield to public transit vehicles at a transit priority signal. The round signal is on top of a regular traffic signal and shows a white vertical bar on a dark background. This allows transit vehicles to go through, turn right or left, while all conflicting traffic faces a red light.

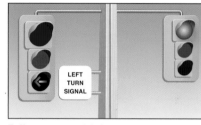

LEFT TURN SIGNAL

Fully protected left turn

Some intersections have separate traffic lights for left-turning traffic and for traffic going through the intersection or turning right.

When a left-turn green arrow appears for traffic in the left-turn lane, traffic going straight ahead or turning right will usually see a red light. You may turn left from the left-turn lane when you face a green arrow. Vehicles from the opposite direction may also be turning left.

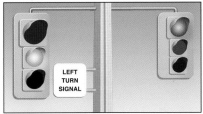

After the left-turn green arrow, a yellow light appears for left-turning vehicles only.

In these intersections, you may not begin turning left after the green light appears for traffic going straight ahead or turning right. If the light turns yellow while you are in the intersection, complete your turn with caution.

Flashing yellow light

A flashing yellow light means you should drive with caution when approaching and moving through the intersection.

After the yellow light, a red light appears for left-turning vehicles only. Traffic going straight ahead or turning right will face a green light or green arrows pointing straight ahead and to the right.

Flashing red light

You must come to a complete stop at a flashing red light. Move through the intersection only when it is safe.

Blank traffic lights

During an electrical power loss, traffic lights at intersections will not work. Yield the right-of-way to vehicles in the intersection and to vehicles entering the intersection from your right. Go cautiously and use the intersection the same way you would use an intersection with all-way stop signs.

Traffic beacons

A traffic beacon is a single flashing light hung over an intersection or placed over signs or on obstacles in the road.

Flashing red beacon

A flashing red beacon above an intersection or stop sign means you must come to a complete stop. Move through the intersection only when it is safe to do so.

Flashing yellow beacon

A flashing yellow beacon above an intersection, above a warning sign or on an obstruction in the road, warns you to drive with caution.

III. Pedestrian signals

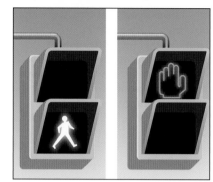

Pedestrian signals help pedestrians cross at intersections with traffic lights. The signal for pedestrians to walk is a white walking symbol. A flashing or steady orange hand symbol means pedestrians must not begin to cross.

A pedestrian facing a walk signal may cross the road in the direction of the signal. While crossing, pedestrians have the right-of-way over all vehicles.

A pedestrian facing a flashing or steady hand symbol should not begin to cross the road. Pedestrians who have already begun to cross when the hand signal appears, should go as quickly as possible to a safe area. While they are crossing, pedestrians still have the right-of-way over vehicles.

At intersections with traffic lights where there are no pedestrian signals, pedestrians facing a green light may cross. Pedestrians may not cross on a flashing green light or a left-turn green arrow.

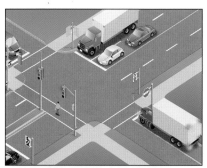

Intersection pedestrian signals

Where there are pedestrian pushbuttons, a pedestrian must use the button to bring on the walk signal. Pedestrian signals give people more time to cross than regular traffic lights. On a busy main road, an intersection pedestrian signal helps people to cross the road safely by signalling traffic to stop. The intersection pedestrian signal has one or more crosswalks; pedestrian walk and don't walk signals; push buttons for pedestrians; and, traffic signal lights on the main road only.

Stop signs control traffic on the smaller, less busy crossroad.

You must observe, obey the traffic rules and use safe driving skills to drive through these intersections. (See Yielding the right-of-way on page 46.)

IV. Pavement markings

Pavement markings combine with road signs and traffic lights to give you important information about the direction of traffic and where you may and may not travel. Pavement markings divide traffic lanes, show turning lanes, mark pedestrian crossings, indicate obstacles and tell you when it is not safe to pass.

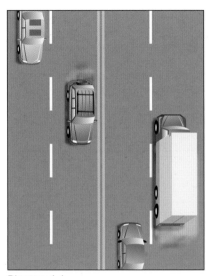

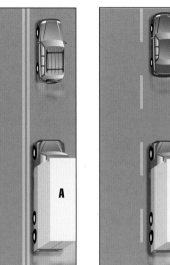
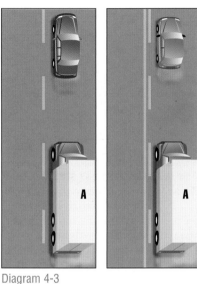

Diagram 4-1
Yellow lines separate traffic travelling in opposite directions. White lines separate traffic travelling in the same direction.

Diagram 4-2
A solid line at the left of your lane means it is unsafe to pass. ('A' should not pass.)

Diagram 4-3
A broken line at the left of your lane means you may pass if the way is clear. ('A' may pass if there are enough broken lines ahead to complete the pass safely.)

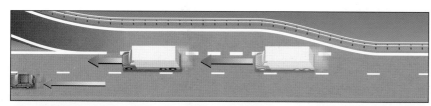

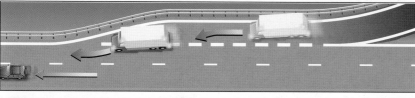

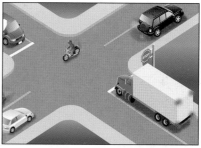

Diagram 4-5

A stop line is a single white line painted across the road at an intersection. It shows where you must stop. If there is no stop line marked on the road, stop at the crosswalk, marked or not. If there is no crosswalk, stop at the edge of the sidewalk. If there is no sidewalk, stop at the edge of the intersection.

Diagram 4-4

Broken lines that are wider and closer together than regular broken lines are called continuity lines. When you see continuity lines on your left side, it means the lane you are in is ending or exiting and that you must change lanes if you want to continue in your current direction. Continuity lines on your right mean your lane will continue unaffected.

Diagram 4-6
A crosswalk is marked by two parallel white lines painted across the road. However, crosswalks at intersections are not always marked. If there is no stop line, stop at the crosswalk. If there is no crosswalk, stop at the edge of the sidewalk. If there is no sidewalk, stop at the edge of the intersection.

Diagram 4-7
A white arrow painted on a lane means you may move only in the direction of the arrow.

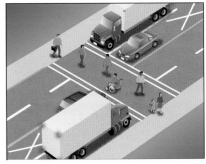

Diagram 4-8
A pedestrian crossover is marked by two white double parallel lines across the road with an X in each lane approaching it, and overhead yellow lights. Stop before the line and yield to pedestrians.

Diagram 4-9

Two solid lines painted on the pavement guide traffic away from fixed objects such as bridge piers or concrete islands.

Yellow and black markings are also painted on the objects themselves as warnings.

Chapter 4 — Summary

By the end of this chapter you should know:

Signs

- The difference between regulatory, warning, temporary condition and information/direction signs
- How to read the symbols and messages of some common signs in each category

Traffic Lights

- The different colours and symbols that appear on traffic lights and what those mean
- How to navigate turns using advanced green lights and arrows
- How to proceed when approaching flashing amber or red lights
- What to do in situations where the traffic lights are not operating

Pedestrian Signals

- What the symbols on pedestrian signals indicate
- What an intersection pedestrian signal is and what to do if you encounter one

Pavement Markings

- How pavement markings are used to control traffic
- What the different colours and types of markings are used to indicate

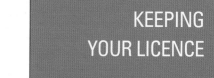
I. Keeping your licence

Ontario has a one-piece driver's licence. The licence card has a photograph and signature of the driver. All drivers in Ontario should have a one-piece licence card. You must carry your licence with you whenever you drive.

Renewing your licence

When your licence is due for renewal, you will get a renewal application form in the mail. Most class A, B, C, E and F drivers are required to pass a vision and a written test at the time of the renewal. Drivers with class A, B, C, E or F licences who are 65 years or older, must pass a vision, written and road test every year. Drivers with a class D licences who are 80 years or older must take an annual vision, written and road tests.

If any tests are required, you must attend a DriveTest Centre to complete the tests and renew your licence. If no tests are required, you must renew your licence in person at a Driver and Vehicle Licence Issuing Office. Take the form into any Driver and Vehicle Licence Issuing Office in the province. They are all equipped to take photographs. You will be asked to sign the form, show identification, pay a fee and have your photograph taken. You will get a temporary licence on the spot if your application and documents are in order, and your permanent one will be mailed to you. You must carry it with you whenever you drive and produce it when a police officer requests it.

If you do not get a renewal application form in the mail when your licence is due for renewal, call the Ministry of Transportation. You are

responsible for making sure you have a valid driver's licence.

If your licence has been suspended, cancelled or expired for more than three years, you will be required to reapply for a licence in Ontario and meet all the requirements of graduated licensing, including passing all the required tests. Only then will you be eligible to reapply for any commercial class licences.

Medical reporting

If you have any commercial vehicle driver's licence other than a class D licence, you must pass a medical examination every three to five years, depending on your age. You will get a notice and a blank medical report form in the mail three months before your medical report is due. You must go to a doctor and get a medical examination. The doctor completes the form. You must submit the form to the Ministry of Transportation,

either by mail or in person. If you do not file a medical report, your class of licence will be downgraded.
- Drivers under the age of 46 are required to submit a medical report every five years.
- Drivers aged 46 to 64 are required to submit a medical report every three years.
- Drivers aged 65 or older are required to submit a medical report every year.

- Drivers aged 80 and older with a class D licence must submit a medical report every year.

Changing your name or address

You must tell the Ministry of Transportation within six days of changing your name or address.

You will need a new licence when you change your address. You can change your address on the ServiceOntario website at

Reason For Name Change	Documentation Required
Marriage	Government Issued Marriage Certificate Change of Name Certificate
Common Law Alliance	Change of Name Certificate
Adoption	Court Order for Adoption Change of Name Certificate
Under the Change of Name Act	Change of Name Certificate

www.serviceontario.ca, or you can take the change of information to a Driver and Vehicle Licence Issuing Office, or mail it to the Ministry of Transportation, P.O. Box 9200, Kingston, ON, K7L 5K4. The ministry will send you a new licence. When you get it, destroy your old licence and carry the new one with you whenever you drive.

If you change your name, you need a new licence. Take the documents you must show (see the chart below) and your current licence to a Driver and Vehicle Licence Issuing Office. A new photograph will be taken. You will get a temporary licence to use until your permanent licence is mailed to you. Carry it with you whenever you drive.

There is no charge for getting a new licence because you change your name or address.

The chart on the previous page shows the documents you will need to change your name on your driver's licence.

Driver's licence laws
It is illegal to:
- Lend your licence
- Let someone else use it
- Use an altered licence
- Use another licence as your own
- Have more than one Ontario driver's licence
- Use a fictitious or imitation licence

II. The demerit point system

The demerit point system encourages drivers to improve their behaviour and protects people from drivers who abuse the privilege of driving. Drivers convicted of driving-related offences have demerit points recorded on their records. Demerit points stay on your record for two years from the date of the offence. If you accumulate too many demerit points, your driver's licence can be suspended.

Fully licensed drivers — Demerit Point System for Fully Licensed Drivers

6 points
You will be told about your record and urged to improve your driving skills

9 or more points
You may have to go to an interview to discuss your record and give reasons

Table of offences

why your licence should not be suspended. You may also have to complete a driver re-examination. If you fail this test, your licence can be cancelled. If you fail to attend an interview, or fail to give good reasons for keeping your licence, your licence may be suspended.

15 points

Your licence will be suspended for 30 days from the date you hand over your licence to the Ministry of Transportation. You can lose your licence for up to two years if you fail to surrender it.

After the suspension, the number of points on your driver's record will be reduced to seven. Any extra points could again bring you to the interview level. If you reach 15 points again, your licence will be suspended for six months.

Here are the demerit points for driving offences.

7 points

- Failing to remain at the scene of a collision
- Failing to stop for police

6 points

- Careless driving
- Racing
- Exceeding the speed limit by 50 km/h or more
- Failing to stop for a school bus

5 points

- Driver of bus failing to stop at unprotected railway crossing

4 points

- Exceeding the speed limit by 30 to 49 km/h
- Following too closely

3 points

- Exceeding the speed limit by 16 to 29 km/h
- Driving through, around or under a railway crossing barrier
- Failing to yield the right-of-way
- Failing to obey a stop sign, traffic light or railway crossing signal
- Failing to obey traffic control stop sign
- Failing to obey traffic control slow sign
- Failing to obey school crossing stop sign
- Failing to obey the directions of a police officer
- Driving the wrong way on a divided road
- Failing to report a collision to a police officer
- Improper driving where road is divided into lanes
- Crowding the driver's seat

- Going the wrong way on a one-way road
- Driving or operating a vehicle on a closed road
- Crossing a divided road where no proper crossing is provided
- Failing to slow and carefully pass a stopped emergency vehicle
- Failing to stop at a pedestrian crossing
- Failing to move, where possible, into another lane when passing a stopped emergency vehicle
- Driving a vehicle that is equipped with or carrying a speed measuring warning device (such as a radar detector)
- Improper use of a high occupancy vehicle (HOV) lane

2 points
- Failing to lower headlight beam
- Improper opening of a vehicle door

- Prohibited turns
- Towing people — on toboggans, bicycles, skis, for example
- Failing to obey signs
- Failing to share the road
- Improper right turn
- Improper left turn
- Failing to signal
- Unnecessary slow driving
- Reversing on a highway
- Driver failing to wear a seatbelt
- Driver failing to ensure infant passenger is secured
- Driver failing to ensure toddler passenger is secured
- Driver failing to ensure child is secured
- Driver failing to ensure passenger under 16 years is wearing seatbelt
- Driver failing to ensure passenger under 16 years is occupying a position with a seatbelt

III. Other ways to lose your licence

Your licence may also be suspended for the following reasons:

Medical suspension
By law, all doctors must report the names and addresses of everyone 16 years or older who has a condition that may affect their ability to drive safely. For example, an addiction to alcohol or drugs is a condition that affects your ability to drive. Doctors report this information to the Ministry of Transportation and it is not given to anyone else. Your driver's licence may be suspended until new medical evidence shows that the condition does not pose a safety risk.

Discretionary HTA suspensions
Your licence may be suspended by court order following conviction for the following:
- If you don't tell the truth:
  - In an application, declaration, affidavit or paper required

by the Highway Traffic Act, its Regulations or the Ministry of Transportation.
- About vehicle liability insurance.
- If you fail to insure your vehicle.
- If you are convicted of some driving offences, included careless driving and driving 50 km/h or more over the speed limit.
- If you repeatedly travel at 50km/h or more over the speed limit. Drivers can be suspended for up to 30 days for a first offence, up to 60 days for a second offence, and up to one year for a third or subsequent offence within a five-year period.

Mandatory HTA suspensions
Your licence will be suspended:
- If you are convicted of failing to stop for a police officer and the court believes you wilfully avoided police during pursuit — that you tried to escape the police. (This is a Criminal Code offence. Your licence will be suspended for a minimum of five years.)
- If you don't pay a traffic fine when ordered by the court.

Administrative driver's licence suspension (ADLS)
Your licence will be suspended **immediately** for 90 days:
- If you fail or refuse to give a breath or blood sample when asked by the police.
- If your blood alcohol concentration is more than 80 milligrams in 100 millilitres of blood (.08).

This suspension takes effect while you are still at the roadside or at the police station. It is an administrative suspension by the Registrar of Motor Vehicles and is separate from any criminal charges or prosecution that may also take place. A $150 administrative monetary penalty is also imposed on drivers who receive an ADLS.

Warn Range suspension
Drivers who blow in the warn range of .05 to .08 pose an immediate danger to themselves and other road users. If caught driving in the warn range, you will receive an **immediate** driver's licence suspension at the roadside.
- for 3 days for a first occurrence.
- for 7 days for a second occurrence and you must undergo a remedial alcohol education program.
- for 30 days for a third or subsequent occurrence in a five-year period and you must undergo a remedial alcohol treatment program and have an ignition interlock condition placed on your licence for 6 months. If you choose not to install an ignition interlock device, you must not drive until the condition is removed from your licence.

A $150 administrative monetary penalty is also imposed on drivers suspended for registering in the warn range.

Your licence will be cancelled:

- If you fail a driver's re-examination.
- If you don't pay your reinstatement fee or administrative monetary penalty
- If your cheque for licence fees is not honoured by your bank.
- If you voluntarily surrender your driver's licence to the Ministry of Transportation or it is surrendered or returned by another jurisdiction.

Criminal Code suspensions

You will receive a one-year licence suspension the first time you are convicted of a Criminal Code offence. If you are convicted of a second Criminal Code offence, your licence will be suspended for three years. A third Criminal Code offence will get you a lifetime

suspension from driving with the possibility of reinstatement after 10 years. Fourth time offenders convicted of a Criminal Code offence are suspended from driving for life with no possibility of reinstatement. Convictions will remain on your driver's record for a minimum of 10 years. The court may order that the mandatory period of a suspension for a Criminal Code offence be extended.

Your licence will be suspended if you are convicted of any of the following Criminal Code offences:

- Driving or having care and control of a vehicle while your ability is impaired by alcohol or drugs
- Refusing to submit to a breath test for alcohol
- Failing or refusing to provide a breath sample for roadside testing
- Driving or having care and control of a vehicle when your

blood alcohol concentration is more than 80 milligrams per 100 millilitres of blood (.08)
- Driving or having care and control of a boat, motorized or not, when your blood alcohol concentration is more than 80 milligrams per 100 millilitres of blood (.08)
- Failing to remain at the scene of a collision to escape criminal or civil liability
- Dangerous driving
- Causing bodily harm by criminal negligence
- Causing death by criminal negligence
- Failing to stop for police

Remedial Measures

There are several types of remedial measures. The mandatory Back on Track program is for all drivers convicted of impaired driving-related Criminal Code offences. For drivers who repeatedly blow in the warn range of .05 to .08, there is a mandatory alcohol education for a second suspension which must be completed within 120 days of the suspension or an alcohol treatment program for a third or subsequent suspension which must be completed within 180 days of the suspension. A Driver Improvement interview is required for drivers convicted of non-impaired driving-related Criminal Code offences. If your driver's licence has been suspended because of a Criminal Code conviction, your licence will remain suspended until you have completed the remedial requirements.

Driving under suspension

You may not drive, under any circumstances, when your licence is suspended. If you are convicted of driving while your licence is suspended for an HTA offence, you will have to pay a fine of $1,000 to $5,000 for a first offence and $2,000 to $5,000 for a 'subsequent' offence. (A 'subsequent' offence is when you are convicted again within five years.) The court can order you to spend up to six months in jail, or you may have to pay a fine or do both. Six months will be added to your current suspension as well. If you are found guilty of driving while your licence is suspended for a Criminal Code offence, you face a fine of $5,000 to $25,000 for a first offence and $10,000 to $50,000 for a subsequent offence within five years. You also face an additional suspension (one year for a first offence; two years for a subsequent offence) under the HTA and up to two years in prison and three years licence suspension under the Criminal Code.

Driving while prohibited

This is a prohibition order under the Criminal Code conviction. When convicted of violation of the order, you will get a suspension of one year for a first offence or two years for a subsequent offence. Courts can order longer prohibition, which will be matched in length by a suspension under the Highway Traffic Act.

Note: Suspended drivers must pay $150 to have their licence reinstated. This fee does not apply to reinstatement following a medical or administrative suspension of your driver's licence.

Vehicle Impoundment Program

If you are caught driving while your licence is suspended for a Criminal Code offence, the vehicle you are driving will be impounded for a minimum of 45 days. This applies whether the vehicle is borrowed from a friend or family member, used for business or employment purposes, rented or leased. The owner of the vehicle must pay the towing and storage costs before the vehicle will be released. This program applies to all motor vehicles including passenger vehicles, motorcycles, trucks and buses.

The Vehicle Impoundment Program makes vehicle owners responsible for ensuring that anyone driving their vehicles is not suspended for a Criminal Code conviction. People loaning or renting their vehicles can verify that a driver's licence is valid by phone at 1-900-565-6555 or online at www.mto.gov.on.ca. You can also get a driver's abstract at Driver and Vehicle Licence Issuing Offices or ServiceOntario Kiosks. There is a nominal fee for each licence checked.

Impaired driving

Impaired driving, which means driving when your ability is affected by alcohol or drugs, is a crime in Canada. Your vehicle does not even have to be moving; you can be charged if you are impaired behind the wheel, even if you have not started to drive.

Alcohol

Drinking and driving is a deadly combination.

All drivers must be able to concentrate on driving. Even one

drink can reduce your ability to concentrate and react to things that happen suddenly when you are driving. With more alcohol in your blood, you could have trouble judging distances and your vision may become blurred. Factors like tiredness, your mood and how long ago you ate and how much, can make a difference in how alcohol affects your driving ability.

The police have the right to stop any driver they suspect is impaired. They may also do roadside spot checks. When you are stopped by the police, you may be told to blow into a machine that tests your breath for alcohol — a roadside screening device. If you refuse, you will be charged under the Criminal Code. The police will also notify the Registrar of Motor Vehicles and your licence will be suspended immediately for 90 days. If the reading on the machine shows you have been drinking, you may be taken to a police station for a breathalyser test. The breathalyser uses your breath to measure the amount of alcohol in your bloodstream.

If you cannot give a breath sample for some reason, the police officer can ask you to let a doctor take a blood sample instead. If you are injured and cannot give your consent, a justice of the peace may authorize a doctor to take a blood sample.

The maximum legal blood alcohol concentration for fully licensed drivers is 80 milligrams in 100 millilitres of blood (.08). Any more than .08 is against the law.

If your blood alcohol concentration is more than 80 milligrams in 100 millilitres of blood (.08), you will be charged under the Criminal Code. The police will also notify the Registrar of Motor Vehicles and your licence will be suspended immediately for 90 days. Even if your blood alcohol concentration

is less than .08, you can still be charged with impaired driving under the Criminal Code.

If you register in the warn range of .05 to .08 on a roadside screening device, you will receive an **immediate** driver's licence suspension at the roadside. For a first occurrence, you will be suspended for 3 days. For a second occurrence in a five-year period, you will be immediately suspended for 7 days and you must undergo a remedial alcohol education program. For a third or subsequent time in a five-year period, you will be immediately suspended for 30 days and you must undergo a remedial alcohol treatment program and have an ignition interlock condition placed on your licence for 6 months. If you choose not to install an ignition interlock device, you must not drive until the condition is removed from your licence. Meanwhile, if there is no one else available to drive and no

safe place to park your vehicle, it will be towed at your expense.

Drugs

Any drug that changes your mood or the way you see and feel about the world around you will affect the way you drive. Criminal Code and HTA suspensions apply to drivers impaired by alcohol or drugs.

Illegal drugs such as marijuana and cocaine are not the only problem. Some drugs that your doctor may prescribe for you and some over-the-counter drugs can also impair your driving. Here are some points you should remember:

- If you use prescription medicines or get allergy shots, ask your doctor about side effects such as dizziness, blurred vision, nausea or drowsiness that could affect your driving.
- Read the information on the package of any over-the-counter medicine you take. Any stimulant,

diet pill, tranquillizer or sedative may affect your driving. Even allergy and cold remedies may have ingredients that could affect your driving.

- Drugs and alcohol together can have dangerous effects, even several days after you have taken the drug. Do not take a chance — ask your doctor or pharmacist.

Consider the consequences of impaired driving

Ontario leads the way in combating drinking and driving through some of the toughest laws and programs in North America, including licence suspensions, heavy fines, vehicle impoundment, mandatory alcohol education and treatment programs and the ignition interlock program. Depending on your number of prior convictions, you may be fined up to $50,000, serve time in jail or lose your licence permanently.

For impaired driving that causes injury or death, the penalties are even more severe. If you are convicted of impaired driving causing bodily harm, you may be sentenced to up to 14 years in prison. Impaired driving causing death can carry a sentence of imprisonment for life.

If you drink and drive and are involved in a collision, you may suffer serious injury or cause serious injury to someone else. Your insurance company might not pay for your medical or rehabilitation costs, or for the damage to your or the other person's vehicle and your insurance costs may rise significantly. You may have to pay substantial legal costs as well.

If you are required to drive on the job, a licence suspension could mean losing your job.

Mandatory alcohol education and treatment

If you are convicted of an impaired driving-related Criminal Code offence, you must complete an alcohol education and treatment program during your licence suspension, also referred to as a remedial measures program.

If you are convicted of a drinking and driving related Criminal Code offence, you must take the impaired driving program called Back on Track, delivered by the Centre for Addiction and Mental Health. The three-part program, which is available across the province, involves assessment, education or treatment, and follow-up. You must pay for the program. If you have not completed the Back on Track program by the time your Criminal Code suspension expires, your licence will be further suspended until you have completed the remedial requirements.

This program also applies to Ontario residents convicted of driving-related Criminal Code offences in any other province of Canada, or equivalent offences in the states of Michigan and New York, as well as to out-of-province drivers who are convicted in Ontario.

If your driver's licence has been suspended for driving in the warn range of .05 to .08 for a second time in a five-year period you must complete a remedial alcohol education program in 120 days from the date of the suspension. For a third or subsequent occurrence of driving in the warn range, you must complete a remedial alcohol treatment program within 180 days from the date of the suspension. You must pay for these remedial programs which are also delivered by the Centre for Addiction and Mental Health. Failure to complete the required remedial program within the specified time period will result in a licence

suspension until the remedial program is completed.

Ignition Interlock

An ignition interlock device is an in-vehicle breath screening device. It prevents a vehicle from starting if it detects a blood alcohol concentration over a pre-set limit of 20 milligrams of alcohol per 100 millilitres of blood (.02).

If you are convicted of impaired driving under the Criminal Code of Canada, you are subject to Ontario's Ignition Interlock Program. After serving a licence suspension, completing a mandatory remedial measures program, and meeting all licensing conditions, you will be eligible to have your driver's licence. At that time, an ignition interlock condition is placed on your Ontario driver's licence, which means that you must install an ignition interlock device in your vehicle.

If you choose not to install a device, you must not drive until the condition is removed from your licence. If you are required to complete a road test while the ignition interlock condition is on your licence, you must complete a road test in a vehicle equipped with the device.

You must apply to the Ministry of Transportation to have the condition removed from your licence. If you have completed the minimum period (one year or three years) without any program violations (tampering/driving without/missed appointment with service provider), the ignition interlock condition will be removed. If you do not apply for removal of the licence condition, it will remain on your licence indefinitely.

If your driver's licence has been suspended for driving in the warn range of .05 to .08 for a third or subsequent time in a five-year period, you will also have an ignition interlock condition placed on your licence for 6 months. However, you do not need to apply to the Ministry of Transportation to have the condition removed from your licence. If you have completed the minimum 6-month period without any program violations (tampering/driving without/missed appointment with service provider), the ignition interlock condition will be removed.

As a vehicle owner, you must not allow a person with an ignition interlock condition to drive your vehicle or you could be convicted of an offence under the Highway Traffic Act. You can find out if a driver has an ignition interlock condition on his or her licence by accessing MTO's website at mto.gov.on.ca or by calling 1-900-565-6555. There is a fee for each licence check.

Driver improvement interview

The other remedial measures program is for drivers convicted of non-drinking and driving related Criminal Code offences who have no previous alcohol-related convictions. You must undergo a Ministry of Transportation driver improvement interview.

If you have not completed the Driver Improvement interview by the time your Criminal Code suspension expires, your licence will be further suspended until you have completed the remedial requirements.

This program also applies to Ontario residents convicted of driving-related Criminal Code offences in any other province of Canada, or equivalent offences in the states of Michigan and New York, as well as to out-of-province drivers who are convicted in Ontario.

Chapter 5 — Summary

By the end of this chapter you should know:

- Your responsibility to maintain a valid driver's licence with the most correct and up to date information
- How the Demerit Point System works for fully licensed drivers
- The driving offences that result in a loss of points upon conviction
- Common circumstances where your licence can be cancelled or suspended
- The consequences that can result from a suspended licence including reinstatement fees, remedial measures, ignition interlock, vehicle impoundment and jail time
- How alcohol and drugs impact your ability to drive
- The consequences of driving while impaired

Chapter 6

I. Ontario's Drive Clean program

Vehicles are the single largest domestic source of smog-causing emissions in Ontario. Drive Clean, administered by the Ministry of the Environment, reduces smog-causing pollutants by identifying grossly polluting vehicles and requiring them to be repaired.

If you own a light-duty vehicle in the Drive Clean Program area (Southern Ontario from Windsor to Ottawa) that is five years old or older and is a 1988 or newer model, you must take your vehicle for a Drive Clean test every two years in order to renew its registration. Light Duty Vehicles manufactured before the 1988 model year are exempt from Drive Clean emissions test requirements. If you are buying a used vehicle that is older than the current model year and is a 1988 or

newer model, the vehicle must pass a Drive Clean test to transfer the ownership and plate it for the road.

Ontario requires all diesel-powered heavy-duty trucks and buses province-wide to pass an annual Drive Clean emissions test. All non-diesel heavy-duty vehicles require annual tests if they are registered in the designated Drive Clean light-duty vehicle program area.

You don't have to wait for a Drive Clean test to do something positive for the environment. Keeping your vehicle well maintained according to the manufacturer's recommended service schedules is an important part of driving clean. For example, if the 'check engine' or 'service engine' lights come on, have your engine looked at by a qualified repair

technician as soon as possible. Otherwise, you could face costly repairs to the vehicle's engine or emissions control system.

Please note that the act of creating, distributing or using false Drive Clean passes is an offence under the Environmental Protection Act. Emissions inspectors who do so can be decertified; vehicle owners will be charged.

For more information on Ontario's Drive Clean program, visit www.driveclean.com or call the Drive Clean Call Centre toll-free at 1-888-758-2999.

II. High Occupancy Vehicle (HOV) Lanes

A High Occupancy Vehicle (HOV) lane is a specially designed lane that is designated for use by certain types of vehicles with a specified number of occupants. It can offer travel time savings to those who choose to carpool or take transit. HOV lanes can move a greater number of people than a general traffic lane, and encourage carpooling and transit use by providing travel time savings and a more reliable trip time. HOV lanes are open 24 hours a day, 7 days a week.

HOV lanes benefit all drivers, not only those who carpool, in the following ways:

- Improves highway infrastructure by moving more people in fewer cars.
- Reduces the number of vehicles on the road.
- Reduces vehicle emissions and improves air quality.

- Helps you conserve fuel, save money (by sharing the cost of driving) and reduce stress.

HOV lanes on provincial highways are reserved for vehicles carrying at least two people (i.e. a driver plus at least one passenger in any of the following passenger vehicles: cars, minivans, motorcycles, pickup trucks, taxis, buses and limousines). Note that large trucks are not permitted on the HOV lanes, regardless of the number of the vehicle's occupants.

The HOV lane is separated from the other general traffic lanes by a striped buffer zone. It is illegal and unsafe to cross the striped buffer pavement markings.

Certain vehicles are exempt from the HOV lane rules. Buses can use an HOV lane at any time, regardless of the number of occupants. Emergency vehicles such as police, fire and ambulance are also exempt from the restrictions.

If you use the HOV lanes improperly, you can be stopped and ticketed by a police officer. You will be required to re-enter the general lanes at the next entry/exit zone.

III. Driving efficiently

Vehicles powered by gasoline and diesel give off air pollutants and gases such as oxides of carbon, nitrogen and sulphur, hydrocarbons and soot. These pollutants affect the quality of the air we breathe, our health, crop yields and even the global climate.

Hydrocarbons and oxides of nitrogen react in sunlight to form ground level ozone, better known as smog. Smog is a major health hazard responsible for respiratory ailments and other illnesses. Oxides of sulphur and nitrogen combine with water vapour to form acid rain, which damages our lakes, forests and crops.

Global warming is the result of too much carbon dioxide and other gases trapping heat in our atmosphere. Global warming could cause average temperatures to rise, causing droughts, crop failures, lower water levels and more frequent and severe storms.

As a driver, you can help to protect the environment from the harmful effects of driving by following these suggestions. Many of them can also save you money.

Fuel saving techniques:
Before you drive:
- Plan ahead. Combine several errands into one trip.
- Avoid driving during rush hours. Driving in off-peak times takes less time, uses less fuel and releases fewer emissions.
- Pay attention to Smog Alerts. It is especially important to follow these suggestions on days when smog is bad.

- Inflate tires to the maximum air pressure recommended by the tire manufacturer.
- Carefully fill fuel tanks; do not over-fill; tighten the cap carefully. Allow room for fuel expansion in hot weather.
- Check the engine oil level; do not over-fill.

Starting up:
- Reduce cranking time. A well-tuned engine should start within 30 seconds. Wait two minutes before recranking if it doesn't start the first time.
- Avoid pumping the accelerator (gasoline engines).
- Use the choke correctly (gasoline engines).
- Use the cold weather starting aids correctly. Don't use them to excess.
- Reduce warm-up idling time after starting.

Moving out:
- Do daily trip inspection before starting a gasoline engine and after starting a diesel engine.
- Move out soon and slowly.
- Drive at low speeds initially. Cold engines have high internal friction until they warm up. High speed driving on a cold engine causes excessive wear and unnecessary fuel consumption.
- Increase speed only when the engine is warm.

While driving:
- Avoid starting your vehicle unnecessarily. A large burst of pollutants is emitted when a cold engine is started.
- Remove unnecessary weight from your vehicle, such as wet snow and winter sand or salt.
- Use your vehicle's air conditioning wisely. Use your windows and vents in city and stop-and-go traffic. At high speeds, using your air conditioning is usually more fuel efficient than opening your windows and reducing the vehicle's aerodynamics.
- Don't 'top-off' the tank when refueling. Spilled fuel releases harmful vapours.
- Manage your road speed. At highway speeds, the faster you go, the more fuel you will use with any type truck on any route. Whenever possible run in the 70-90 km/h fuel-efficient range. Faster or slower than that and consumption of fuel increases.
- Match gear to speed. You should always be in a gear where your RPM is as low as possible, at least 200-300 RPM below the governed maximum. You cannot get good fuel consumption unless you combine efficient engine speed with efficient road speed.
- Minimize idling by shutting down the engine whenever possible, except in very cold weather.
- Maintain a steady cruise speed, the lowest steady speed that will permit on-time arrival at your destination.
- When approaching an upgrade, open the throttle smoothly and shift down only when engine speed makes it necessary.

Operating in traffic:
- Anticipate how traffic conditions are changing and what other drivers will do. By looking ahead, behind and to the sides, maintain an efficient speed or make smaller speed adjustments.
- Select lanes with the smoothest traffic flow.
- Select lanes for efficient speed.
- Maintain a space buffer between your truck and vehicles ahead. This will minimize speed changes and braking. Letting your buffer shrink and expand will make your driving smoother and therefore more fuel efficient. The buffer will also enable you

to make safe lane changes without slowing down.

At the garage:

- Regular maintenance will keep your vehicle running at maximum efficiency, reducing the fuel you need to buy and the pollutants your vehicle emits.
- Keep your vehicle's engine well tuned. Worn spark plugs, dragging brakes, low transmission fluid or a transmission not going into high gear can increase fuel consumption substantially.
- Follow the recommended maintenance schedule in your vehicle owner's manual to maximize fuel efficiency.
- Have any fluid leaks checked by a specialist to avoid engine damage and harming the environment.
- Keep your tires properly inflated to reduce your fuel bill, emissions and tire wear.

- Have your vehicle's alignment checked regularly to reduce uneven tire wear and fuel consumption.

Fuel consumption techniques summary:

If you learn and practice the following techniques, you'll be well on the way to good fuel consumption:

- Use good starting procedures.
- Get going as soon as you can.
- Control your idling.
- Be an RPM miser.
- Use progressive shifting.
- Maintain efficient engine speed.
- Manage your road speed.
- Operate efficiently in traffic.

IV. Mandatory Vehicle Branding Program

Under the Mandatory Vehicle Branding Program, insurers, self-insurers (fleet owners), auctioneers, importers, salvagers and anyone who deals in used vehicles, are required to determine whether severely damaged and written off ('total loss') vehicles they insure or obtain should be branded either 'Irreparable' or 'Salvage'. They must notify the ministry of the brand through a Notification of Vehicle Brand form. The ministry applies the brand to the vehicle's registration information so that it will appear on the vehicle permit, vehicle abstracts and the Used Vehicle Information Package (UVIP) for that vehicle. The brand identifies the condition of the vehicle to potential buyers. This is how the program helps to protect consumers buying used vehicles.

If your vehicle sustains severe damage and is written off by your insurance company, your insurance company must notify you and the ministry of the brand requirement. If you do not receive a claim settlement through an insurance company, you must have the brand determined by an authorized mechanic at a Type 6 Motor Vehicle Inspection Station. The ministry website has a list of these facilities — visit mto.gov.on.ca for details.

There are four brands:

- A vehicle which has never had a brand applied in Ontario automatically has the brand 'None' applied to its registration documents. However, this does not mean that the vehicle has never been damaged in a collision, was never branded in another jurisdiction or was not rebuilt prior to the mandatory branding program.

- The brand 'Irreparable' means that damage to the vehicle was so severe that the vehicle can be used for parts or scrap only. It cannot be rebuilt, and it can never be driven in Ontario.

- The brand 'Salvage' means that the damaged vehicle can be repaired or rebuilt. It cannot be registered as fit to drive in Ontario. Once the vehicle has been repaired or rebuilt, and if it can pass a structural inspection to ministry standards, the owner can obtain a Structural Inspection Certificate and have the vehicle branded as 'Rebuilt'.

- The brand 'Rebuilt' means that the vehicle has been previously branded as 'Salvage', but has been rebuilt and has passed a structural inspection to ministry standards. If the vehicle can pass a safety inspection (Safety Standards Certificate), the owner can have it registered as fit to drive in Ontario.

Motorcycles that have been written off must be branded 'Irreparable'; they cannot be branded 'Salvage'.

Trailers, traction engines, farm tractors, mopeds, motorized snow vehicles, street cars or motor vehicles with a model year of 1980 or earlier are exempt from the mandatory branding program.

V. Sample questions for Class A or D knowledge test

1. When travelling at less than the normal traffic speed, what lane should you use?
2. What colour light identifies a snow removal vehicle?
3. Except when passing, how many metres (feet) must be maintained between commercial vehicles travelling in the same direction on a highway outside a city, town or village?
4. What must the driver of a truck do before entering a highway from a private road or driveway?
5. When a truck becomes disabled on a roadway during the period when lights are required, at what distance must flares or reflectors be placed to the front and rear of the vehicle?
6. The maximum trailer length is?
7. When uncoupling a semi-trailer unit, what is the next step after lowering the landing gear?
8. What should tractor-trailer drivers do while rounding a right curve on a highway?
9. What is the maximum length of any combination of vehicles?
10. When must a driver perform a vehicle inspection?
11. When backing to couple a semi-trailer, the fifth wheel opening must be in direct line with?
12. When a load projects 1.5 m (5 ft) or more over the rear of a vehicle, what should it be marked with?
13. When entering a freeway, you should signal, then?
14. What does the gross weight of a commercial vehicle mean?
15. You should, under all conditions, drive at a speed which will allow you to?
16. All vehicles, including load, are limited to a height of?
17. Who is considered an "operator" under Commercial Vehicle Operator Registration (CVOR)?
18. What factors affect the maximum gross allowable weight of a commercial vehicle?
19. A driver performs a vehicle inspection and discovers that some of the brakes are out of adjustment. What is required of the driver?

Chapter 6 — Summary

By the end of this chapter you should know:

- What Ontario's Drive Clean Program is and how it works
- What High Occupancy Vehicle (HOV) lanes are and how they work
- Techniques for driving efficiently and saving fuel
- What the Mandatory Vehicle Branding Program is and how it works

Conversion chart

Imperial to Metric Converter

From	To	Multiply By
inches	centimetres	2.54
miles	kilometres	1.61
feet	metres	0.31
pounds	kilograms	0.46
miles per hour	kilometres per hour	1.61

Metric to Imperial Converter

From	To	Multiply By
centrimetres	inches	0.39
kilometres	miles	0.62
metres	feet	3.28
kilograms	pounds	2.21
kilometres per hour	miles per hour	0.61

Personalize your licence plates — with two to eight characters, as well as a great choice of colour graphics. Then you'll really stand out from the crowd.

Turn the page to find out more.

NOW THERE ARE MORE WAYS THAN EVER TO EXPRESS YOURSELF!

WE'RE HELPING YOU BUILD CHARACTERS.

Now you've got extra choices when creating your personalized licence plate. We've introduced seven and eight characters. So you've got even more to work with — a minimum of two characters and right up to eight. Just think of the possibilities.

Every personalized plate is one of a kind. No one else can have the same plate as yours.

For more information and to order your personalized plates, call 1-800-AUTO-PL8 (1-800-288-6758).

**Or visit the ServiceOntario website: www.serviceontario.ca
Or drop by your local Driver and Vehicle Licence Issuing Office
Or one of 70 ServiceOntario kiosks.**

Gift certificates are available too.

Graphic licence plates are a hit! And now there are more than 40 choices available. Support your favourite Ontario sports team, community or arts organization, professional group or university. Or select a timeless icon like the loon or trillium.

For a totally unique look, add a colour graphic to a personalized plate with up to six characters.

So express yourself — with colour graphics and personalized licence plates.

For more information and to order your plates, call 1-800-AUTO-PL8 (1-800-288-6758).

Or visit our website: www.mto.gov.on.ca
Or drop by your local Driver and
Vehicle Licence Issuing Office
Or one of 70 ServiceOntario kiosks.

Gift certificates
are available too.

ADD SOME COLOUR WHERE IT COUNTS.

Other MTO Publications for you

Copies of this handbook and others may be purchased from a:

- Retail store near you;
- DriveTest Centre;
- Driver and Vehicle Licence Issuing Office; or
- Publications Ontario

50 Grosvenor Street

Toronto, Ontario

M7A 1N8

- www.publications.serviceontario.ca

or by calling

(416) 326-5300

or 1-800-668-9938 (toll free)

(416) 326-5317 (fax)

Prepayment required by cheque or credit card — VISA or Mastercard. You may also pay with a certified cheque at DriveTest Centres.

Handbook prices are subject to 5% G.S.T. and 5% shipping costs. Please add 10% to your total purchase to cover G.S.T. and shipping cost. Map is subject to 5% G.S.T., 8% P.S.T. and 5% shipping costs. Please add 18% to your total purchase to cover G.S.T. and shipping cost.

The Official Driver's Handbook
$ 14.95
ISBN 978-1-4249-4041-7

The Official Motorcycle Handbook
$ 18.95
ISBN 978-1-4249-4043-1

The Official Truck Handbook
$ 18.95
ISBN 978-1-4249-4045-5

The Official Bus Handbook
$ 18.95
ISBN 978-1-4249-4047-9

The Official Air Brake Handbook
$ 18.95
ISBN 978-1-4249-4049-3

The Official Ontario Road Map
$ 2.95
ISBN 0-7794-4210-5